from Fear to
Freedom

Removing
The Fear

Ifedayo Greenway

& 11 Fearless Women Transforming Through Truth

REMOVING THE FEAR

Printed in the United States of America
ISBN: 978-0-578-36515-2

Ifedayo is available for speaking engagements, book signings, and workshops. Send your requests to ifegreenway@igandmore.com

Special discounts are available on bulk quantity purchases by book clubs, associations and special interests groups. For more details email: ifegreenway@igandmore.com

This book is dedicated to the She Unveils Movement. To each and everyone of you that are committed to unveiling your story, telling your truth and living a life LESS impacted by fear, I salute you. Yes! Yes! Yes Change!

TABLE OF CONTENTS

Foreword

So here we are, we meet again. Not the same time, but it's always a specific place. Our encounters are often inconvenient and crippling in nature. I am a skilled expert on the subject matter, so it was only befitting to write from this lens. Rarely identified by name and often glossed over as something else, I am the mistress of stagnation and the first cousin of procrastination. The one thing you struggle to break away from. I am the shadow that lurks and invades relationships, new opportunities, and your day-to-day decisions—derailing the hopes and dreams of anyone that crosses my path.

I have been in the background of your life for years, watching you exude with confidence on the outside while the mere thought of me suffocates your internal ambition and blinds your vision of the future. Causing shortness of breath every time you take a step towards the unknown. Paralyzed by overthinking and bound with doubts about tomorrow. Yes! I'm deeply rooted and accompany many on this ride we call life. I am your fear!

Please know that this level of exposure is bittersweet. I am filled with pleasantry when I think of my role in this book and what I have been able to accomplish in your life. However, I know that I will succumb to the bitter and pungent after-effects of your freedom from my hold after you read this book. The courageous writers in *Removing the Fear: A Truth Journey from Fear to Freedom* have chosen to defy the odds of what a normal interaction with me looks like. They have made the conscious decision to feel my presence and do it anyway. Despite my influence, they have chosen to strip me of my power and use it for their strength. Denying their urge to flee and taking a stance to fight. No longer confined by the shackles of 'what if.' Giving themselves the freedom to be delivered from my reigns and release their truth, and they are challenging you to do the same. The compelling stories of each writer will cause you to examine the parts of *you* that have been left undone because of me.

Since this book is a truth serum, please allow me to share mine. I am a signal for concern. My goal was to distract, derail and even destroy you. As I secured my position and reached my comfort zone in your life, I gloated in the way you fed my energy and marveled over how you glorified my existence by giving up so much to soothe me. But I know this book is our crossroads.

The truth of the matter is...

Removing the Fear: A Truth Journey from Fear to Freedom is a call to action because it's time for you to decide.

Choosing yourself requires putting in the work. Relinquishing control and stepping outside of your comfort zone. Stripping away the anxiety and breaking down the walls of indecisiveness. Confronting consuming thoughts of your past and re-centering your focus on the future. Refusing to fall victim to the debilitating thoughts of inadequacy. Acknowledging that where you are is not where you're meant to stay. Releasing what was and accepting what will be. Causing you to channel a new way of thinking and ultimately propel you into the next step of your journey.

So, which one of us will you choose? Me or you?

Signed,

The Silent Inhibitor of Your Change

The Fear of Letting Go

Ifedayo Greenway

"Ma'am, are you alright?" I heard the question escape the lips of the driver as he connected my car to the hook and chain of the tow truck; he was preparing to pull the inoperable lump of steel from my garage. What I felt in my heart was manifesting through tears as I stood watching him. I was nearly hyperventilating as I anticipated the final roll out of my driveway. My soul felt an ache that many people would never seemingly feel... over a car.

I was the essence of what it meant to be the proud owner of a motor vehicle that I cherished. It was probably everything opposite of grandiose in the eyes of others. Still, for me, I was driving in the lap of luxury. The pearl white, four-door sedan adorned with tan leather seats and gold trim was the first automobile I had paid off and owned with evidence of a clear title locked away in my safe box. I purchased a second one years later, but I rarely drove the new car. Instead, I would jump in *old pearl* (yep, I named it as if it was a part of the family) and drive it all day, every day. This car was my ol' faithful. I had plans to drive it until the wheels fell off, and I almost did just that. With over 320k miles on the odometer, the engine finally conked out. After it broke down, I contemplated getting it fixed. But after calculating the cost, I quickly concluded that the repair fees were more than she was worth. However, I wasn't ready to part ways with it. So, I parked her in my garage, where it stayed for over a year. It camouflaged well with the other containers and boxes I had justified storing away. I never complained about the space it was taking up, although I could have used it for my other car. For me, old pearl was a part of the indoor structure, and it had earned its right to be there.

I struggled with surrendering what I deemed an irreplaceable kinship connection. That car meant so much to me because it was loyal. The seat seemed to hug and comfort me like an old friend whenever I sat in it. Even when it was broken down and seemingly worthless, I placed a high value on it. It was a permanent fixture at a time in my life when everything around me seemed to be ever-changing. Although unusable, old pearl was the one thing that I could count on to be there when I needed to see something that represented stability, even if it was a false representation.

Up until that point, I had endured so much loss. I had been divorced twice, estranged from a close group of sister-friends, had left my job, church, and home of many years to move to a city where I had no family roots, connections, or friends. But, as the garage door lowered and old pearl could no longer be seen, my emotions attached to giving up the car exposed a broader view. I realized a bigger picture that had become a barren pattern down through the years. But, of course, I didn't fully understand it that day. Still, subsequent years of holding on to broken-down relationships, un-serving mindsets, and even material things (unworn clothes and shoes) that no longer served a purpose in my life illuminated an underlined fear that had been ingrained in me; the fear of letting go.

Fear is defined as an unpleasant emotion triggered by the perception of real or imagined danger. But what could I possibly have envisioned as a potential risk or perceived threat of relinquishing things, especially when they served no purpose? From a literal standpoint, letting go symbolizes the release of something. Emotionally and psychologically, it is when I accept the things I cannot change and take action to do something about the things I can. Unfortunately, the fear of letting go meant that even when I had the power to alter the outcome, I allowed my imagination and embedded lies to convince me that somehow nothing would ever be different for me.

I had normalized holding on to stale and outdated blessings. What I clinched on to had convinced me that I didn't deserve anything with an up-to-date status. New doors only opened for other people. Fresh blessings were for everyone else and not for me. It felt like I always got right to the brink of a new job, new house, or healthy relationship, only to be met with denial, delay, or rejection letter. So, I held on to the obsolete for fear that letting go would leave me empty and deprived. I lived in the shadows of the perceived unfairness of life. I was not trusting that my journey of living would ever be equitable and return to me something greater than what I contemplated giving up. I would rather keep what was broken and of little to no value than accept that I was worthy enough for its replacement. Holding on to the *something I had* was vastly superior to the possibility of ending up with nothing at all.

Let me answer the obvious question: what was it that I needed to let go of? First, I needed to part ways with the people-pleasing assignments that had become weighted and unproductive work. Saying yes to the invitation to work with or for others with vague motives, the tasks or speaking engagements I knew I was supposed to decline, but I agreed to because I desired to feel busy, wanted, accepted, or relevant. Second, I needed to untie the knots with people with whom I had embittered entanglements and walk away from places that no longer served my success. Third, I had to relinquish the *I'd rather have something than nothing* syndrome that kept me sitting in the painful place of the familiar rather than trusting that better was on the other side of the release. Most importantly, it was imperative for me to unhand the unpleasant emotion packaged as the fear that fed my impulse to hold on to all of it.

Please understand there are two sides to the fear coin. In the Bible, II Timothy 1:7 tells us that "God has not given us the spirit of fear." Therefore, some will argue that we are not supposed to feel it at all. I disagree. That scripture says that God has not given us the spirit, but there are times when *feeling* it is necessary. Fear can be healthy or unhealthy. When the distressing feeling shows up in a fight or flight incident, the perfect response causes a person to act and react accordingly. On the contrary, when it is the thing that drives the emotional imagination and causes me to be mentally immobilized by unproductive fantasies of worst-case scenarios, it no longer has a healthy motive. Rather, it is the poison to what would otherwise be a fruitful tree, the internal collision that could potentially paralyze me from ever walking effectively in my purpose-driven life. The spirit of fear is its embodiment or essence, which is different from sensing it in a necessary moment that may save a life. My mind had integrated and was intertwined with the lies of trepidation, and it weaved a mental web of dysfunction. It fed my twisted perception of a limited God and caused me to hold on to things and people far past their expiration date. I never trusted that what was coming was better than what was going. If I let go of the man who was masterfully manipulative and who constantly cheated, would a better one want me? Would I ever be able to find someone that just effortlessly did it for me or made me feel the way he made me feel? I refused to accept goodbyes, fought to hold on to the familiar, and justified dragging out-of-season things into new seasons. I had a false sense of loyalty to assignments and people who had no problem discarding me when they were fulfilled or needed to move on. *That* was the fear that needed to be removed.

Pulling back the layers of my struggles presented me with a multi-pronged issue that I needed to explore.

There were times when what I toiled with was not fear itself. Instead, it was the life I knew that I could have if I would just let the fear go.

This truth would come to uncover a deeper layer to this phenomenon. What was I *really* afraid of? Well, the answer was twofold. It was the idea of being stuck with mediocracy because I was either (a) too afraid to let *average* go or (b) fearful of what it would feel like to embrace first-class. I was scared to lose and even more terrified to win. I wasn't always frightened by the worst-case scenario. In some instances, the best possible outcome made me uneasy. It caused me to refuse to live a life beyond the proverbial wall of apprehensive excuses. It was the question on the opposite end of, *what if I don't get a better return* spectrum. The double-edged sword that said, but *what if I do*. I remember years ago, talking to a friend after I completed a book project and saying, "What if I don't do well with book interviews and selling this book?" Her response was, "What if you do?"

I normalized things not working out for me. So, could I respond appropriately if it did? Was I capable of walking in the win? Would true happiness cost more work and effort than I was willing to put in? Would I be able to properly steward the blessing on the other side of the release? I wanted to live a life less impacted by the fear of letting go until the subject matter struck a chord with a more intimate truth that I wasn't ready to face or receive. I thought I was gaining traction with the mandate of dismissing until God recently demanded I give up the one thing that I had been holding on to the longest and walk away from a twelve-year relationship as I knew it. Yep, He required me to give up what I never thought I would be able to surrender and put in the work to heal and arrange my life for the happily ever after that.

The truth of the matter is...

Letting go hurts! Releasing what was necessary for me to move forward was (and is) very painful. Reminders of the old seemed to be commingled in every part of my life, and there were days when I craved and wanted it back. There were times when I second-guessed my decision to part ways with what previously satisfied and stagnated me all at the same time. I had moments when I secretly had to talk myself out of reclaiming my comfort zone. My humanity was conflicted. I so desperately wanted to stop the ache caused by letting go of "what was." But the conflict in my soul quickly reminded me that would ultimately be self-sabotage for what *is* to come. I spent too long mourning over what God had strategically rejected and pushed out of my life. I repeatedly negotiated with Him to keep the things or people that He had clearly revealed needed to go. And since I'm already out there on a limb with my truth, the deeper revelation is that if I had released some things sooner, the pain probably wouldn't have been as immeasurable and seemingly beyond baring.

It wasn't until I completely opened up to this chapter of my life that I understood that letting go is not the end. Yet, it is the pivot required to take the next step in my change journey. God is reforming my life, restoring my faith, and reinventing my perception of Him. It is my new beginning! But please know this. Although it is the inception of new life, severing ties requires follow-up work that is quite intense. God's promise to give me abundant life (John 10:10) didn't come with a guarantee that overflow would always be handed to me with no effort on my part. Seeing the manifestation of bountiful requires a fight. There are times when the delay between the release and the recovery causes me to question everything I believe. But let's be clear, God is not a liar. He can't lie. Although I get weary from having to grapple for what feels like should come easily by way of His assurances, the reality of my story is that I have to fight! The way I see it is, if He promised it and it ain't coming easy (which nothing rarely does), I need to square up with life and go to blows for my better. I have to keep writing the books when they don't seem to be selling, wrestle to hold on to my hope when life seems to be winning, maintain my posture of patience while I'm in the holding pattern for purchasing my dream home, and allow my heart to heal and believe in love again after it has taken a serious beating. Challenging my limited beliefs meant that I needed to spend more time with my therapist to unpack where the illogical thinking originated. No's, and denials didn't mean that I wasn't worthy of better; it meant that I had to take action and mentally and emotionally fight for it. The delays are the pathway to a level of humility that teaches me to appropriately respond and makes me confident that I will steward every forthcoming blessing with a heart that is more profound with gratitude.

For many of you reading this, *letting go* is the next step in your process. You cannot bypass or circumvent the necessary order of ordained operations. It is time for you to cut the hovering cords that you have dysfunctionally connected to your children. Release the toxic and underserving relationships that are killing you softly on the inside. Walk away from the stagnant places that are counterproductive to your forward progress. And most of all, comprehend that your *better life* is waiting for you to disconnect from the fear that keeps you committed to your average one.

As you read through the coming chapters, I admonish you to find yourself in the stories of these courageous women. I hope you acknowledge your fears and the lies they have embedded. I pray that you welcome in a new sense of freedom and trust that your journey of removing the fear is the conduit to the truth of the matter in your own life.

The Fear of Living

Kenya Allen

Taking my life is the best option because I don't think things will ever get better for me.

These thoughts probably sound crazy to the person living their best life but not to me. Even as a woman of God, I still had no clue what living the *best life* looked like. I know the Bible says that Jesus came that we would have life and have it more abundantly. But from my reference point, the only abundant life that I saw were the people in church. Well, they looked like it anyway. As a person who is gifted and assigned to pray for others, I prayed for prosperity for them, but I was totally void of the manifestation of what I thought growth and success could be for me. The moments I felt most alive was when God and I had our time together in worship. But when worship ended, I reverted into a lifeless person.

Over the years, I've asked myself what on earth was I here for? I knew there was more to life than just waking up, getting out of bed, and going to work; that was just existing. I'm talking about aligning my existence with walking in my purpose and enjoying an abundant life. It seemed that nothing survived around me, so I had no other reference points. My mother died when I was just four years old. My father was a very abusive man who left right after my mom passed, leaving any hope for him and his love dead. After my mom died, I moved to Portsmouth, VA, in a four-bedroom project apartment with my grandmother. It was ten of us, five adults and five children. We didn't have much (there goes that just existing); however, my grandmother made it work. She had the strength of ten thousand men to me. She would always say, "God is keeping me; God is my provider." I would stand in front of her, thinking, *why do we have to walk everywhere we go? My friends' moms have cars; why hasn't God provided us with one? Why are we living like this?* Now again, she made it work, and she did the best she could with what she had. Our apartment was always clean. She wore some of the most beautiful suit coats. And her hats set her apart, and she had one for every outfit. I was well kept too. We were some of the cleanest dressing people ever seen. We had food to eat, and oh yea, she could cook too. The smell of her food would open our noses and put a smile on our faces, and the taste would leave us wanting more. She made something out of nothing without me having to know how she did it until I got older. However, even with us having the things we had, I knew there was more to this thing called life; I just felt it in my gut. I got a glimpse of this good life when I visited my Papa's (my grandfather) house in New Jersey. The bishop is what he is called to this day because that's his position in the church. I was the oldest grandchild to my Papa, and I loved it. My Papa had this big house with hardwood floors, a big stove with a large kitchen, and a lot of rooms. It had a piano and a basement with two additional rooms. When I visited, I thought I was in heaven. I would dance with my socks on so I could slide across the floor, waiting for my Papa to come through the door and yell, "Hey, Mickey." Mickey was my mom's nickname, but he gave it to me when she passed. Me and him were really close. We took trips to Canada and Hershey Park; I enjoyed every minute of it.

My life took a turn when I was sixteen. The void of not having my mother shifted me into a place of rebellion. There were no more visits to New Jersey because of my hardheadedness; I lost contact with my Papa because I wouldn't listen to his wisdom. I didn't feel wanted or needed by him. I refused to hear what he or my grandmother told me. Right or wrong, I was determined to make my own decisions. I had my son Dondrell shortly after. I was numb to the strains of what my existence meant. I was a high school dropout and a single mom with no job. I had nothing to offer my son as far as I was concerned.

Don't get it twisted. I loved my boy; I just didn't know how to be a mom. I survived with the help of my grandmother (I was still living in her home) and sixty-five dollars a month in child support. Yep, sixty-five whole dollars a month, oh, and food stamps. How could I forget about those? And if my life wasn't already hard enough, I got pregnant again twelve months later with my daughter, Deshara. At this point, my grandma told me that I had to go because I wasn't doing anything positive for myself. She contacted some of her manager friends from public housing, who called me in to do paperwork, which started me getting into my own place. I moved into a two-bedroom apartment with two children and later obtained a job working at a childcare center. I worked Monday-Friday, from six am to six pm. I would walk my children to my grandmother's house and then walk to work. Life had gotten harder and harder for me; being a single mom was tiring and definitely not what I imagined as a better life. I felt like I was just working to pay bills. No car. No motivation. I was depressed. I wanted my childhood back and often prayed, "God, please take me back. Take me back to when my mother was living, and I could see her smile. Take me back to when my father was sober, spinning me around in his arms. I'm sick of it, God; God, do you hear me?" It felt like God was ignoring my pleas for a greater quality of life, so I took matters into my own hands.

I had to do what I had to do for me and mine. And I did. You name it; I got it; cars, clothes, money, I had it. And it was all from drug money. To me, I had arrived; I was finally living. At least that's what I thought until my freedom was threatened. On a Saturday morning, I opened my door, and there were nine policemen pointing guns at me. They sat me down at the kitchen table and told me my charges. I was facing ten years of incarceration in federal prison. Whew, talk about being numb, dumb, and devastated all at the same time. There were no words to explain my emotions. How could I serve ten years in the penitentiary? Who would take care of my children? I had no parents, my grandmother was too old, and I was still not communicating with my Papa. What was I going to do?

I wanted to literally stop living because, at this point, I had nothing to live for. Because death was all I knew, death is what I resorted to. I came up with a plan to kill my children and then myself. That night while my babies were sleeping, I took the gun from out of the closet, sat in the middle of my bed, and waited for the right time to end our lives. Then suddenly, my daughter walked into my room holding her brother's hand. This three-year-old little girl, wise beyond her years, rubbing her eyes and walking towards me, said, "Mama, God said he's faithful to you." Tears began to roll as my son climbed onto my bed, helping his sister up as well. With his thumb in his mouth, he looked at me and said, "Yeah, mommy, he is throwing the gun away, mommy." I grabbed and rocked my babies in my arms and cried out to God, "Lord, help me!" And He did just that. I gave my life back to Christ on a Sunday morning.

That Monday, I received a phone call from the detective that had my case (by the way, there were actually two people who had my case, one is a partner at the church I attend. If you are reading this, I love you). That phone call changed my life. The deep voice on the other end says to me, "Ms. Allen, we no longer need you to turn yourself in, have an amazing life and take care of yourself and your children. Oh, and Ms. Allen, somebody was praying for you because this doesn't normally happen this way." And he was right, you either do your time, or you snitch, and I wasn't doing either. So, my prayer to God was that if He got me out of prison time, I would serve him the rest of my life. I didn't promise Him that I wouldn't sin anymore or make any mistakes, but I would serve him. And that is just what I did.

I went back to school and received my high school diploma. I studied Early Childhood Education in college. After that, I became a director of a private child-care center. From there, I became a teacher. However, with all of my accomplishments and accolades, there were still problems in my life with men, my children, and my family. I suffered from bouts of depression, anxiety, and constant worrying about different things. And there were times when I still wasn't happy. Don't get me wrong, I was grateful for what God had done, but I still was not walking in my destiny, and it was because I was afraid to do so. I had come to the realization that I was scared to live because I didn't know how.

The truth of the matter is...

It has taken up until now, yes, I said it, *now*. As I write and you read, for me to say I, Kenya Allen, am currently living because I'm experiencing life beyond everything that was physically dead or emotionally assassinated in my life. Some may assume that because of all that I've been through and for all that God has done, my decision to live (now) is late (at best). However, I have been pushed to live. For God has put me on the minds of people that'll give me exactly what I need and when I need it. Again, I desired to be pushed to think better, move better and do better. No matter what was going on in my life, the bad was never God's fault. Nothing that happened to me was God's fault. Even the things that I had no control over. I was going through because of the decisions that I made. I did it to myself. Me! My thought life caused me not to live. Thoughts like: *I wouldn't be anything. I'm not a good mom. I'm not good enough. I don't qualify. I'm not smart enough.* What a (wo)man thinks in HIS heart, so is HE. The scripture says, "train up a child in the way he should go, and when he is old, he will not depart from it." And while the Word of God didn't depart from me, I, however, departed from it when I believed the negative thoughts that bombarded my mind. Once those thoughts got empowered by me, they, in turn, blocked my blood-borne right (to live an abundant life) that Jesus Christ himself gave me. My thoughts of fearing death held me hostage, to just exist. But God has the final say-so over me! I dug deep and decided to change my bloodline by focusing on the promises of God. Believing who I am and whose I am. I am a child of the Most High God. I can do *all* things through Christ, who strengthens me. I decree and declare by the authority of Jesus Christ that we shall Live and Not Die but walk out the plan and purpose that God has for our lives.

I am now living.

The Fear of Embracing Freedom

Tahisha Pernee' Thompson

Anxiety was rooted in me at birth. My mother was in labor with me for 72 hours. There was no technology to tell if the baby was in distress as it is today during that time. She was afraid something terribly wrong was happening at any given time, causing severe anxiety; this stress was genetically transferred over to me. I internalized worry to be a part of my natural being at an early age. I normalized it to control my emotions and as an excuse not to accomplish a task. I don't think she realized the impact it had on me. The sound of a siren terrified me when I was growing up. My stomach would immediately ball up into knots, and I would get sick to the point of nausea. The news of a family member or friend passing away would cause me to immediately start to regurgitate. To be honest, my mother's anxiety started with her mother.

I can remember my grandmother often said she had a nervous feeling and something terrible was going to happen. An uneasiness entered the room, and we would sit frantically waiting by the phone or a knock at the door for the bad news. This irrationality taunted me throughout my childhood with a suspicion that something detrimental would overtake me. When I became an adult, that trait intensified. I was afraid to experience new things, watch horror movies, ride rollercoasters, go places by myself, and just do things that young adults did. I hid behind the shadows of others because I was scared of who I was and who I would one day be. I had dreams and aspirations but was anxious to pursue them because I was dreadful of failure and what others would think of me. The fact that I had low self-esteem was a significant factor, and I allowed it to sabotage me for a long time.

This embedded apprehensiveness trickled over into my marriage life. From day one, I thought the worst was going to happen. The thoughts of infidelity, divorce, not being the right size or pretty enough, or my husband passing away and leaving me haunted my daily existence. I had friends who had experienced divorce and lost their husbands, and I didn't want that to be my story. So, when my husband began to have health issues, anxiety controlled and consumed me; I was afraid of becoming a widow. I would lay awake many nights worrying about the what-ifs. I prayed and pleaded with God not to let my nightmares be my reality. I don't know if I was frightened of being a widow or scared of unmasking my identity.

It was a beautiful Wednesday morning; the sun was sitting perfectly in the sky. I had celebrated my 47th birthday and 14th wedding anniversary just a few days before with my husband and girls. We drove to Canada and experienced the best family vacation ever. We laughed, reminisced, and talked about how excited we were for the next season of our lives. Finally, I could breathe and release some of the built-up anxiety I had carried since we were married. For the first time in our marriage, I felt at peace and looked forward to spending the rest of my life with him and our daughters. We were preparing to celebrate Jada being a Senior in High School and Jami'yah, a 7th Grader. The time of being empty nesters was closer than it had ever been. Life was perfect - until I received a dreadful phone call to come home because my husband was lying on the ground, non-responsive, in my neighbor's yard. The frantic drive from my job to our neighborhood seemed more like hours than 17 minutes. My heart was pounding, and I was dreadful of the unknown. I tried praying, but it was hard. I knew I needed reinforcement, so I made several phone calls to my parents, pastor, and best friend. They could hear the panic in my voice and immediately began to pray against the worst in hopes of a favorable outcome. I needed to be reassured that everything was going to be alright. As I turned into the subdivision, I saw people standing in the street, a fire truck, police cars, and an ambulance. All of the things that terrified me as a child were right in front of our house. I jumped out of my SUV running and praying that I would hear my husband say, "Baby, I am okay; I just got overheated." But that was not the case. My superhero was on the ground, lifeless, as the paramedics worked profusely to pump life back into him. On Wednesday, September 6, 2017, the love of my life suddenly transitioned from his earthly home to his eternal home. I was numb, and I felt as if my life had ended with his. There I was, standing amongst neighbors and friends, a widow at the age of 47. A million things began to run through my mind. *This can't be happening to me. God, please tell me I am dreaming. How am I supposed to live without my husband?*

We became one when we were married; therefore, I was not my own. I couldn't fathom a life without him; I was the one that was afraid to be alone. My heart broke. No one in my inner circle had experienced such a significant loss. The ones who I hid behind could no longer hide me. I was exposed and had to face my biggest concern. Every Wednesday after, I would lay in a fetal position waiting on God to take me where my husband was. I didn't want to leave my daughters but facing my reality of a new normal was more than my heart could bear. I felt as if the world was on my shoulders. In one day, I went from being a helpmate to sole provider, and it was a responsibility I didn't want to take on. I panicked at the thought of it. I would wake up in the middle of the night with anxiety attacks trying to remember if I paid all of our bills. I was petrified that ends would not be met because my therapist recommended taking a year off work due to post-traumatic stress. There was no way this was the life that was predestined for me.

I was discombobulated to the point that I didn't recognize myself. Whenever my husband and I would go out, he would introduce me as "His wife." He rarely called me by name. At home, it was "Baby." If he called my birth name, that meant there was trouble in the camp. His friends and family referred to me as Nelson's wife or Mrs. Nelson. Even when I tried to interject and say, "Ta-hisha," I felt unheard and that my individuality wasn't significant. I can honestly admit that my husband's death left me with a lot of questions and very few answers.

Let the truth be told, Nelson's death awakened a fear of independence that lay dormant in my soul. I was reluctant to seek out my true identity. Here I was free to be all that God had called me to be, and I didn't want any parts of it. The act of embracing freedom was not a desire to be released from my husband or marriage but to be free from my insecurities. I was happy in my marriage, but the sacred vows of "death do us part" made me realize that my entire identity was tied to it.

We are identified as either female or male from birth, and a label is placed on us. I was the first child, granddaughter, great-granddaughter, and niece when I was born. I was known as Hosea and Liz's oldest child. It was rare that I was called by my name, Tahisha. In adulthood, I had more labels: mother, widow, minister, intercessor, and friend. I was no longer Nelson's wife or Mrs. anything. The thought of exploring the real Tahisha paralyzed me to the point of being stagnant. I became complacent and comfortable not embracing the opportunity of freedom. I am free to walk into my purpose without reservation and the desire to seek approval from others. Freedom to tap into my wildest dreams of being a successful entrepreneur. Again, I fell victim to fear when I realized I was no longer invisible.

The taunting of my past happy life lurked through my soul, manifesting in night sweats, sleepless nights, and self-medicating. The sad thing about it is that I could still function as if everything was okay. I was an imposter. I lived for validation, wanting to be accepted and fit in. Again, because of my low self-esteem stemming from my childhood, I grew up thinking I was ugly and fat and that I would never be good enough. I tried to throw myself in circles to be *seen*. I drowned in my insecurities. Self-Sabotage was my greatest enemy and friend. But deep down inside, I knew there was more. But I didn't know how to get to it. And yet there was still a voice inside of me screaming, "Let me out." It was the echo of my authentic self calling me to live!

It felt as if I was in William Shakespeare's play, Hamlet. I was in a dilemma that needed immediate answers; *To be free or not to be free*? Would I have the courage to peel off the many masks I wore proudly? Or would I live in bondage and miss the opportunities God has predestined for me?

The truth of the matter is...

While removing my mask is necessary, the weight of freedom for me is heavy. The fear of the unknown had me incapacitated in my own negative self-talk. I realized that I was afraid of what was on the other side of pain. However, to my surprise, it was greater than I imagined. And for the first time, I no longer care about how others perceive me. I don't have to enter a room in despair with my head down and have to change my disposition because of the company I'm in. I can now look in the mirror and actually admire the beautiful woman I see. I honestly know I am fearfully and wonderfully made.

And as I began this healing journey, I now dared to shed the heavy layers of doubt, shame, and condemnation I carried for so long. Instead, my peace and well-being are my primary focus. I am so grateful to God that I did not lose my mind!

My smile is radiant not because it's forced but because it is genuine. I am ALIVE, and I praise God, who kept me through the most painful season of my life. I had to put on my "big girl panties" by making tough calls and fully embracing all of Tahisha. I have flaws, and it's okay.

Finally, and this was a biggie for me; I had to stop looking for the approval of others for my life decisions. I had to be delivered from my insecurities. The mandate on me requires that I be totally honest with myself. And because I am now free, I can walk others through their journey to freedom.

I choose to no longer be invisible or hide my true identity. When I enter a room, an immediate shift takes place because I can be who God has called me to be. I walk with boldness and confidence, knowing who I am and whose I am. I have taken charge of my choices, and I love Tahisha, the woman. I am a great mother; I am a successful entrepreneur, and most importantly, I am loved.

Look out, world, my name is Tahisha Pernee,' and I am freely embracing Me.

The Fear of Falling in Love with Me

Nicki Peacock

"And they overcame him by the blood of the Lamb, and by the word of their testimony."

Revelation 12:11 KJV

Testimony:

The existence or appearance of something provides evidence or proof.

I don't believe I woke up one day and decided not to love myself. It must have come from somewhere; something happened that was so intense that I internalized it as not being good enough or not feeling worthy. And while I don't hate myself, however, I started to deem myself as unlovable. I thought about it, and the Holy Spirit revealed to me where it all started. The moment when I planted the seed of unworthiness, and when I told myself that no one loved me.

My mother, Aleta (RIH), and father, Floyd, weren't together any longer. Both lived separate lives without the responsibility of raising their children. My older sister went to stay with my dad's mom. I lived and was raised mostly by my mom's older sister, Aunt Noy (RIH). My mom went off and lived her life traveling from state to state. I didn't really see much of her, and my dad lived locally, but I did not see him at all. There were times when he would call and say he was coming to pick me up, and I would get so excited. I'd pack my overnight bag and wait on the porch for him, and he was a no-show. Each time he would call, he gave an excuse of why he didn't show up the last time and how this time would be different, and I believed him. And again, there I was, waiting on the porch disappointed.

I think I was around eleven years old when he said he wanted me to stay at his house for the summer and that he was really coming this time. I don't know why my aunt thought it was a good idea to allow me to stay that long, but she agreed. I was excited, so I packed my bag again and waited all day Saturday. This time he actually showed up late, but he showed up. I hopped in the car, and on the way to his house, we stopped by McDonald's (which is still my favorite). He let me get whatever I wanted from the menu, then drove the rest of the way to his apartment in Oceanview. He had a girlfriend, and she had two daughters, which she treated differently from me. When we got inside his place, he told me to go into the room, close the door, and not to come out because he had friends over. I sat alone in a room eating my food, trying to figure out what I had done wrong. The next day was the same thing. McDonald's and then in the room alone because he had company over. If I needed to use the bathroom, I had to crack the door and yell over the music and them talking to let him know I needed to come out. I would go to the bathroom and then right back in the room. Usually, this was the routine for the three-day weekends. During the week, he would go to work around six in the morning and leave me in the house alone most of the time with no food, no money, no nothing. I would find money around the house, walk to the corner store, and get snacks until he returned. Sometimes he would take me riding, but I had to wait in the car by myself if he stopped somewhere. After a few weeks of this, I told him that I didn't want to stay at his house alone every day. His girlfriend told him about a recreational center he could take me to during the week while he was at work. He told me about it, and I agreed; I just wanted to get out of the house. The next day, he wakes me up at 5:30 am to get dressed. We get in his work truck and pull up to the center around 6:30 am. He tells me to wait at the front door until they open. I said, "okay," and got out and watched as he drove away. I read the sign on the front door and saw that it opened at 9 am.

As a child, I couldn't understand what was going on. Why would he leave me out there by myself for hours? I began to feel like trash being thrown away, like I meant nothing to him. He abandoned his own child. This was before cell phones, so I was literally sitting outside the building in the dark, waiting for the center to open. Don't get me wrong; I would have a good time while I was there just being around people. But morning after morning, my dad dropped me off outside the center alone. I felt like something was wrong with me because my mom wasn't around, and my dad seemed to not want me around either. After a few weeks of being left alone, I was so depressed and unhappy. I called my Aunt Noy collect on a payphone. When she answered, I told her as calmly as I could that if she didn't come to pick me up, I would run away and she would never see me again. She came, and I didn't see my dad again for another ten-plus years.

Throughout the years, I guess I learned how to deal with the fact that most of my life, I've been alone. As an adult, I'm by myself, which means I spend a lot of time alone. I'm also an over-thinker. Sometimes I can't tell if God is isolating me for a reason because He is working on me or if I'm isolating myself because I don't like what I see and I'm attempting to hide. However, because of the amount of time I spend by myself, I do find out more things, and it has forced me to deal with myself. I have been living a life where I didn't really like me that much. I love me because it's easy to love somebody and not really like them, but I don't really like me too much.

Not liking myself means putting me last and doing things I really don't want to do for other people in fear of them walking away because I say no. I isolate myself from others because I don't wanna get attached; I don't want to be forced to be rejected again. It's me attempting to keep busy in order to not deal with whatever I am going through. I blame myself when people leave or when things don't go my way. I'm hard on myself because I'm not who I thought I would be or where I want to be today. The constant picking myself apart daily was my normal routine. I had more bad days than good because I could see the good in everybody else, but I am blind to the good in me. Oh, I am good at praising God for other people's victories and blessings but terrible when it comes to me because I do not believe I deserve the same happiness. This has turned me into a people pleaser. I continuously want to please everybody, so they don't walk away. It's almost like keeping others happy, so they can't see that I am unhappy. It now makes sense why it's easy for me to isolate myself, why I prefer to be in my room and why I think of McDonald's as my comfort food. I never really realized how the little things affected me in such a huge way, or even how one thing can dramatically change how I view myself. I am good at compromising what I really want to say or what I want to do in relationships in fear of being abandoned. Mostly in a panic of them leaving me like my dad did. It's making me relive every morning being dropped off on the curb, watching my dad drive away. It's me always asking God, "What's wrong with me?"

It's the constant reminder of never being good enough for love. It's not wanting to let go of the familiar disappointment in the past because of the unknown that lies ahead. Basically, I allow my past to stay in my future. It's convincing myself that I trust God completely when I really don't! Man, I give good advice, but I do not like taking it. It's allowing those seeds of negativity to sprout in my thoughts daily, and it is a constant battle between my heart and my brain. There is literally a war going on in my mind, which causes me to overthink everything. So it's difficult to enjoy the little things. I find it difficult to like anything about myself because I'm too busy comparing myself to others.

The truth of the matter is...

I remember getting up one morning and deciding that I liked myself and everything that came with me. And that waking up each morning is a blessing and a gift from God. It also means that God still has a plan for my life. God did create me in His perfect way, so in reality, I'm perfectly created. I've learned to accept who God created me to be and stop judging myself based on other people or how those people treat me. There were times when things were happening, and people would leave, but I now know that's not my fault - there's nothing wrong with me. People are people, and I just accept who they are and move on. Either they fit in my life, or they don't. And I continue to tell myself this. I have learned how to speak life and encourage myself. I have learned to be ME!

When I give full control to God, He decides who stays and who goes in my life, not me. That's not my job. My job is to be who he created me to be!

I'm still learning how to better love myself, even now, writing this. It's a daily task to tell myself I matter and remind myself that I am absolutely fabulous. God's timing is the only timing that matters. Telling myself that I'm where I'm supposed to be in life, and there is nothing wrong with me. I affirm that I am loved. But I will not lie; loving myself is easy; it's the liking part that takes some effort. But it's an effort that has to be done daily. And the more time I spend with myself, the more I start to like me, and the more that I like me, the more I fall in love with myself.

Can you imagine falling in love with yourself and what that will feel like? I felt you smile because I'm smiling writing this. And God is smiling too because you just realized that you can fall in love with yourself. Falling in love with you means being content with who you are at this very moment today. Once you fall in love with yourself, you'll start to let yourself off the hook a little bit and enjoy the small things about yourself. Extend yourself some grace to be imperfectly you. You will begin to realize that the things that make you are the things that you fell in love with to begin with. Those little imperfections you see - it's okay if you didn't turn out quite the way you thought you would. Just begin to thank God for the small things in life, the subtle things He has placed in you. When you do, thank God that it may not be the life you imagined for yourself, but just know His ways are perfect, and you're exactly who and where you are supposed to be. Those unimportant things that used to bother you won't bother you anymore. Accept them; in fact, it'll make you appreciate your value more, and then you'll stop watering yourself down and walk in an authentic way. Honey, bask in your own ambiance.

Breathe in and breathe out; that's you smelling like fresh air. When you start to fall in like with yourself, it's like enjoying your favorite thing, every second of every day. You will experience an awakening - realizing who you are and what you have to offer. It's going to be amazing when you know your worth and decide not to dim your light to make other people shine.

Again, trust God's timing.

The easiest part about loving yourself is that God already loves you so much. And when you love God, when you fall in love with God, his love is so easy because God is love, and love is God. So when you begin to love yourself, please invite God into your heart and ask Him to clean out those places you thought didn't need any cleaning. Get bold and ask Him to uncover things that you covered up. Then ask Him to go in and perform surgery on the things that you put a Band-Aid on. Repeat after me, "Lord God, create in me a clean heart and renew a right spirit within me" (Psalm 51:10). You have now given God permission to do what only He can do, and that's be God.

You do the work, but God does the heavy lifting.

If I had to sum up or paint a picture of what loving yourself looks like daily, my mind goes to that movie, "50 First Dates." It's the one with Adam Sandler and Drew Barrymore. Adam's character (Henry) falls in love with Drew's character (Lucy), who has short-term memory loss; she can't remember anything that happened the day before. So, every day he has to remind her that they are in love. Every morning she has to learn how to love him all over again. And that is what loving yourself looks like. Remind yourself every day that you love you. If it's affirmations, do that. If you have to write down a song that you need to hear, do that. If it's a poem you need to write to yourself or whatever you need to do to remind yourself as soon as you wake up that God loves you, do it. Remind yourself that you love you too. Some days it's gonna be easy. Some days you won't even have to remind yourself. But there will be those days you might have to tell yourself 25,000 times before you leave the house. Whatever it takes is the effort that needs to be put into the heavy lifting part. The Bible says faith without work is dead. (James 2:17) So this is the work.

The Fear to Believe in Me

Arlene Kidd

From birth to the age of fourteen is a blur; I only remember bits and pieces. Some may think it's strange that I have little recollection of my life, although I wish I could. The things I do recall are mostly negative. I blocked a lot out, but I know I lived in an abusive household. I would dread seeing my father leave the house to work because my mother would get furious while he was away.

Often, I would go to my dad for anything I needed or wanted. But, for the most part, my mother's physical and verbal lashings were for the darndest reasons. I was punished with the bristles of my hairbrush because I was up after bedtime combing the tangles out of my hair. I often wondered why a loving relationship with my mother didn't seem possible. I was unsure she felt any affection for me.

Years of experiencing this unpleasant behavior resulted in me developing envy towards other mother and daughter relationships. Whether it is my friends and their mothers or just random encounters. This lack of affection from the woman who birthed me introduced an emptiness in my very being. Learning that she grew up with an alcoholic father, I could only imagine the lack of love she may have encountered herself. Positive affection was sure to be lacking when her siblings were shot at by her very own father. The scars that this alone must have caused. She was never probably allowed to ask why. Knowing this small portion of her childhood information has led me to conclude that the family abuse must run deep. How else can I define all the maltreatment towards my siblings and me?

My mother did not hesitate to take a belt and whaling away or send us to the tree for a switch until we bought one long enough that sufficed. Mind you; the punishment was always greater than the offense of painting my nails in the house, walking up the stairs too hard, talking amongst my siblings after being sent to bed, or not providing her a glass of ice water at the time she wanted. All of these minor things seemed to require a harsh punishment. If her response wasn't physical, then it was verbal; I swear nothing I did was allowed, nothing I did was ever enough for her.

It didn't appear I was worthy of any compliments. Rarely if ever, did I hear good job, nice work; you can do it, everything will be okay, or it will work out. I'm certain the lack of positive praise growing up has surely impacted how I must have thought of myself. In actuality, it translated to a negative belief in myself.

I feared doing and or saying anything to just about everyone. Painful statements replayed in my mind… *you aren't good for nothing, you can't do anything right.* All of which left me discouraged to try. Ultimately these statements became my truth and what I really felt about myself.

In my early teens, my mother was diagnosed with lupus. She was already injecting herself with insulin two or three times a day due to her diabetes, on dialysis, and now this. So, my hopes of this mother and daughter relationship turning for the better were appearing bleaker and bleaker. But, unfortunately, no one really gave any real explanation of what any of this meant. So, I was left to process it without any guidance again.

With my siblings out of the home at this point, it was just my parents and me. I could not grasp what was happening, and I desperately needed my mother. And although I had older siblings that I may have learned a thing or two from, I rebelled against them; I didn't care to hear from them. I wanted my mother to explain and help me understand what was going on with her. Truth be told, I don't believe my mother was capable of meeting the motherly expectation that I so badly desired.

As the months passed, I started to feel empty, broken, and confused. Needless to say, I began to fill that space with things I believed would make me feel whole; smoking, drinking, hanging out, and there was the boyfriend. I was fifteen and about to become a mother. This time I decided I was keeping my child. Yes, I said this time, it was my second pregnancy. I dreaded having this conversation with my parents.

"So, you didn't learn from your first mistake? My parents asked me.

I was apprehensive, but I had no other choice but to respond. And when I did, silence fell in the room. Their next words were, "You cannot stay here!"

A few weeks or so later, I commence to leave home, as my parents are seated on the couch observing my every move, but with no reaction, no encouragement, just their silence. I wanted them to say, "Don't go; we can work this out." But that was just wishful thinking on my part as the door closed behind me.

At fifteen, I was so fearful; the reality that someone would need me to be what I wasn't scared me. *How will I know what to do? How will I feed my child? How will I pay for shelter for my unborn child and me?* All those questions I asked myself. I was so ashamed with little to no answers. It ultimately resulted in me leaving high school, living with my boyfriend's grandmother, and later his parents and siblings, pregnant and with no real plan.

I didn't know if I could, but on January 19, 1987, I pushed my daughter out of me, and then I cried tears of joy and uncertainty. But I was reminded that this was a life-changing moment, and there was no time for a pity party. *I can do this*, I said to myself, *there's no turning back now.*

I was doing the mother thing, and I was doing it well, along with the help of her aunts and father. For her father and me, this parenting thing was all new. Then, approximately three months later, I had a moment when I had a complete meltdown. My daughter just wouldn't stop crying, and something came over me that I wanted to shake her. All I can remember saying to myself then out loud was, *I will not be abusive like my mother*! Something about that comment, my stance, caused another light bulb to go off within me. After that, I was reminded daily so that I would not chastise my daughter unnecessarily.

I was about six months in being responsible for a life, and my boyfriend and I started to bump heads. I knew the environment I did and didn't want for my daughter. I expressed the importance for us to move, and there was no movement. So, I moved back home for a short period, and for the majority of those days, my mother was in the hospital. My daughter remained with her father and his family. I established employment and was ecstatic over my Burger King job. I felt some sense of accomplishment. I went to work every day to make a living for my daughter and me.

I met a young lady who offered to rent me a room; I accepted. I moved out of my parents' home again, but with my head up this time. I took on a second job which caused me to spend less and less time with my daughter. It wasn't until her father said he was planning to move to Florida and was taking our daughter with him that I woke up. I was not letting this happen. I had to get over not believing in myself enough to be a mother and to do it solely on my own. I had to muster up enough faith and confidence in my own capabilities.

One Sunday afternoon, while staying with yet another friend and his family, I received a phone call from my father. "Hello Daddy, how are you? Is everything okay?" He answered, "Yes, however, I need you to come home and help with your mother." I rendered a long sigh. *Wait one minute; now you need me?* Of course, I didn't say it aloud, but I sure thought it. "Daddy, I hear your request, but can I think about it?" I had a little time to decide during her hospital stays but my mother was declining rapidly. Between diabetes, lupus, and kidney failure, it took a toll on her body. Finally, I decided to move home. I did not realize the responsibility ahead of me. I worked during the day, and my dad worked nights several times a week.

My evenings with my bedridden mother and a two-year-old were very challenging. She was still trying to control me with her words since she couldn't beat me physically any longer. Nevertheless, I remained focused and did what I was asked. However, the strengthened belief that I was building a life for my child and me while out of their home was starting to diminish.

"Bring me the phone!" She would holler. And when I did, it resulted in the police knocking at our door shortly after. So going forward, I would give her the phone per her request, but it was unplugged. When she figured it out, more bellowing came, "Plug this phone in, you kids make me sick!" It took everything in me some days to keep it together because my sanity was tested.

With the built-up animosity I had towards her, there were days I wanted to neglect her just as she did me. I was potty training my daughter and changing pampers for my mother at 50 years old. However, I never followed through with the thought, and I remained diligent to the assignment as her caregiver.

May 1989, I was seventeen and had a conversation with my father: "Daddy, is there anyone else we can get to come and help with momma? This is overwhelming?" Although we had spoken on these things before, I really didn't feel I could handle much more. My mother's mouth was still wild, which continued to cause me to question my belief in myself.

Precisely, three weeks after our conversation, my mother went into the hospital again. I don't know how long she was there, but I recall the hospital calling to speak with my dad. I saw the worry on his face as he departed to go see her. This day was more vivid than most as I paced the floor waiting for a call or him to return home. I had an uneasiness in my belly, and my patience was wearing thin, so I called the hospital to inquire about my mother, but they refused to provide any information.

Finally, I heard my father at the door. When I greeted him, I noticed he was accompanied by my aunt. Instantly, I knew. Mother had succumbed to her illnesses. News of her transition caused sadness but more for what my father had to endure. I was numb until the funeral, and then a sense of relief fell upon me.

I forgive my mother, but I carry pain for feeling like I never really had one who believed in me.

It was only when I was able to take care of my mother in spite of the negative stuff that I took a different perspective about believing I could do something right. Even then, I did so with some reservations and many hiccups. For a long time, I used a lot of excuses to keep from moving forward. Anything I could conjure up that kept me from bettering myself, I would find it and use it. I have even talked myself out of job opportunities. Who does that? Me.

The truth of the matter is....

I've suppressed my feelings for a long time. This is what's keeping me stuck. I want to be delivered so I can move on. I have to accomplish something for myself to stop feeling like my past is holding me back. I see others walking out their dreams, which I admire, and I know it could be me if I would just believe in myself more.

So, although plenty of lies were embedded in my spirit over the years, I am pulling them out from the root. I am choosing to believe!

"For as he thinks in his heart, so is he."

Proverbs 23:7

The Fear of False Narratives

Alva Kershaw

I was 15 years old the first time I heard, "you ain't nothing, and you will never be nothing. You are just a project girl. I don't know who you think you are to believe that you're going to college." So, hearing those ugly words again - 20 years later, from another man I had allowed into my life, was jarring. "Who do you think you are; nobody cares about what you think?"

He had already manipulated large sums of money from me throughout our relationship under the guise of togetherness. We were supposed to be building a life, raising a family. But, on the day that I turned 12 weeks pregnant, the mother of his other newborn daughter called to announce her birth and demand that my boyfriend parent her child. It seemed that the negative narrative of my life was on repeat, *you ain't shit*. This story continued to show up like the proofs you get after taking pictures, stamped so everyone notices.

The argument and subsequent fight in my hospital room, only four hours postpartum, started because he needed to avail himself to sign our daughter's birth certificate. He'd be required to furnish his identification card to sign the document. But producing the ID would undo the years of deceit he'd woven into our relationship.

In the next few weeks, my life would change in ways that I did not want to accept or could anticipate. My daughter's entry into the world was scheduled, and my labor would be induced on Oct 13, while my mother was convalescing in the hospital. After my mother's surgery and my daughter's birth, the hospital served as my safe place. It was home, where my mother was, and she was home for me. My mom had a hard time waking. The doctors considered a tracheostomy because of her dependence and extended time on the ventilator. I went to her bedside, pleading with her to awaken. The very next day, when I arrived in her room, she was alert and eager to have the tube in her throat removed so she could speak.

Talking with my mother brought some relief, but the veil of sadness that covered me didn't lift. I chatted with her about her grandbabies but omitted the terrible parts. In fact, I told no one about the violence the day my daughter was born because the vibration of *you ain't shit* had silenced me. Everyone was overwhelmed and needed my mother to get better. We were hopeful, though we knew her recovery would take lots of care and consideration. Unfortunately, the devastation that followed had not been scheduled. She contracted a bacterial infection, resulting in sepsis, which caused her organs to fail. Eighteen days after the birth of my daughter, on Halloween, October 31, my mother literally gave up the ghost, leaving me here with *the-just-in-case-you need-them* insurance policies that she left hanging on the front of her dresser.

I had no time to break down or even feel sorry for myself. I only had time for fleeting moments of recuperation in the days ahead, pausing long enough to focus on immediate tasks that demanded my attention. For me, slowing down too much was threatening; the grief might catch me, or my daughter's father might catch me, and I feared that I'd die, too.

Most days after my mother's death was like walking through fog. Hours mimicked dreams as I slithered between sleep and wakefulness; the feeling of euphoria made it difficult to determine if my reality was, in fact, real. Everything felt like a nightmare, and I could hardly distinguish between living and hovering above my body. I wasn't thinking of dying; I just had a hard time deciding to get up and live each day. But my infants' tears would remind me that I had no choice. So, I began caring for my children and helping them do what they couldn't do for themselves. Unfortunately, my ex made my days difficult because he wanted to focus on us. I was insistent that our relationship shattered that day in the hospital room. My logical mind understood that my mother was no longer here, but my heart decided there had to have been some mistake.

This episode of my life that was playing couldn't be real. Momma had only shared the insurance policies with me in *a just-in-case* scenario. My existence mirrored shattered glass, and I was truly in an existential emergency. While I was too spiritually mature, at that point, to consider that this was God's plan for my life, I chose to believe that I had made a mistake. As a matter of fact, that was the only conclusion that allowed me to edit the tragedy that had become my daily grind. If I had made poor choices, then that is what I could control. And then there were a host of things that I could only cry about, like the decision not to ask my mother to postpone her surgery or when I failed to ask the skilled nursing facility to return my mother to the hospital sooner. And then there's the mistake of getting involved with and settling down with an insane person; prayerfully, there'd be an opportunity for me to attempt a course correction. But no matter how I felt about my mistakes, none of them could be undone. And that vibration of, *you ain't shit and never will be*, continued to create distorted figures when I looked at myself in the mirror.

I realized that this combination of events with my ex and my mother awakened fears inside me in a way that I had never known. I had been raised in one of the most notorious urban housing projects in this country, and I never recalled this kind of fear. I was single and alone, and for the first time, I was without the support and wisdom of my mother. Her absence left me exposed; I had not faced those words of condemnation without her. They were easily dismissed because she was there to help me refute them. "You can do whatever you put your mind to," was her mantra for me, and these words lived as long as she had been around to repeat them.

There was a limit on my ability to see beyond the here and now, and I needed hope that whatever previous seeds I had planted would bear fruit. I had no voice for God. I went through the motion of feeding my children and providing for their basic needs. One of my sisters moved in with me. It was good for a time because we absolutely needed each other; otherwise, we may not have been able to survive our mother's transition. Losing her caused us to lose pieces of ourselves, and to keep from slipping away completely, we held tight to one another. Daily, our collective grief grew worse, albeit for reasons unique to each of us. My anxiety and grief became one-in-the-same.

The next few months were plagued with the tasks of managing my mother's affairs: planning her funeral, clearing personal belongings from her home, and supporting her significant other. My mother's sister and I met at my mother's home and cleaned until dark. We were diligent in completing the tasks, but it took more than either of us really had to give.

After the fight with my ex, I called my daughter's paternal grandparents requesting that they help me get my keys and personal items from their son. They were elderly, married for more than 50 years, and accustomed to their son's negative behavior. I would later learn he had a history of violence and sociopathy. He started stalking me the day after my mother's funeral. This man harassed me, called me more than 200 times a day, and showed up in odd places. I know this seems exaggerated, but it's all true. The greatest tragedy, though, is that I couldn't call my mom and tell her what was happening.

Because we weren't married, we went to court for custody. The courts discovered that he was calling me excessively when they subpoenaed my phone records because he lied to the judge, who was eager to believe that I was the angry Black woman. The adjudication process assisted in belittling me and stripping away the bit of dignity I had salvaged. This too became a supporting narrative, elevating that vibration, *you ain't shit, and don't you ever forget it.* I was accused of being a bad mother, and the Guardian Ad Litem believed him. The judge believed him when he accused me of being crazy and deranged. He told the judge that I was upset because he didn't want to be bothered with me and had chosen to engage in a relationship with his other child's mother. He told the judge that I was using our child against him and would not allow him to see her because of my jealousy. It did not matter that I made every accommodation possible. I was ridiculed in court for withholding our child from visitation to make matters even worse. I felt invisible inside those judicial chambers. My pleas for protection fell on deaf ears. I was the one who was followed and chased in vehicles everywhere I went. There was a tree in my yard I had cut down because I would come home, and he'd be standing behind the tree. I love to sit outside, but I was so traumatized by his constant presence that I could not sit outside for years. It has only been in recent months that I have been able to use my porch again. Once he came for a visit with our daughter, we got into an argument, and he pulled me down three cement stairs. My oldest daughter is still traumatized from seeing the blood on me. I fought back, which I know he did not expect. He was arrested but released immediately. He has threatened to kill me, and the courts, despite my constant reports, failed to help me. Their only concern was that I was impeding his visitation.

I was fully immersed in a full-blown, physically aggressive bout of domestic violence. I was denigrated beyond belief. And he went through great lengths with his relentless pursuits to inform me that he was in charge. My anxiety about him got the best of me. I was afraid to go to my car at night. If I'd left something, it would stay there until the morning. This might sound trivial, but I had a newborn, which made it a significant inconvenience. I sometimes had friends follow me home because I feared that he'd be standing in my backyard. I had the hardest time watching my dog while she relieved herself because I was afraid that he'd attempt to hurt either of us. He could not stay away. The police did not deter him, and violence did not deter him. The only time I got relief from the harassment was when he was incarcerated for things unrelated to me. During the investigation that was ordered by the court for the purpose of revealing my criminality, I spoke with a detective. She warned me that he was very dangerous, had over 14 aliases, and had committed domestic violence crimes and other things in multiple states that she could not share. She warned me that I needed to be very careful. This fueled my anxiety and my grief.

The truth of the matter is...

I was grieving, primarily, the loss of my mother. But there was more to it than that. It was like I was walking on eggshells for a long time. I lost my best friend, my safety net, the day my mother died. Losing her was not the first life-altering grief I'd experienced, but it was the most impactful. Growing up in the projects proved to be traumatic. I'd done everything that I possibly could to escape the toxicity of that experience. I went to private school with the hope of procuring a better future for myself. I started working at 15, eager to earn my way out. I even got married (but later divorced with my first child). And when my mother's voice was silenced, I heard what I had been able to stave off for damn near a lifetime; you *ain't shit, and you never will be. No matter what you do or where you go, you still won't be shit.*

It felt as if every failure and challenge I'd ever had put me in my place. "Who are you, and how did you get here? Who'd you think you were to try and escape your fate?" And for a long while, I was too tired and frustrated and anxious to answer. Then, finally, I gave up, in a sense. It was not that kind of beautiful, willful, and deliberate surrender that you hear about in books. It was the *you-have-nothing, none-of-it-matters, and you-can't-change-it-anyway* type of letting go.

I made many sacrifices to shed the skin of trauma. I had gone to higher learning institutions where I was not wanted and was repeatedly told that I was not good enough. I had a master's degree and was licensed to practice independently in the state. I was even employed by the government at the time of this cluster of unfortunate events. But none of it seemed to matter. None of my accomplishments as a daughter, a wife, a friend, a graduate, a professional, a volunteer, or a mother seemed to be enough to overcome that embedded stamp that caused everyone to notice that failure is simply proof that I was not valuable. I was labeled for all to see.

After I recognized the false narrative and my fear, I was overwhelmed to admit the presence of multiple unpleasant narratives tethered to the original. And I was being labeled as *not good enough* had become painfully repetitive throughout all of them. No matter what happens, I will be required to answer the question: Who do you think you are? And in doing so, it is imperative that I understand my intentions and motivations. Other people initially decided that because of my upbringing, the premature deaths of my father and brother, and being raised in a single-mother household that I was the cause and not the solution to a problem that I did not create. I was determined to prove them wrong. I was determined to retake the portraits and remove the stamps that everyone could see.

This process of learning, unlearning, relearning, and editing the narrative has been heavily ladened with pain and disappointment. However, if I am being fair to myself, there have been good times. I have a lifetime of love and friendships that have contributed to my ability to recover from that not-so-pretty kind of surrender. I would be less than honest if I were to say that the ebb and flow that has resulted from exposure to trauma and other people's ideas about it has ceased to be a part of my life. The more honest part is accepting that it took some time, perhaps more than I want to admit, to recover the pieces of myself that departed when my mother died. The truth is, I did find my voice, and

I know it when I hear it. Not only do I follow it, but I fight for it. I struggle and toil amidst the chaos of those initial voices that sometimes make more noise than my own. In these moments, I get still and quiet and let it happen. I let the truth come in. I allow the memory of my mother's voice to vibrate through my own, "You can absolutely do anything that you set your mind to do. Every journey begins with a single step. Get up and get on with it."

The Fear of Authenticity

Sandra L. Parker

In April of 2021, I started working on a book project with my mentor and coach. As she was preparing me to move forward, she said to me, "Tell me your story." As I began to share, I felt vulnerable. Finally, she persuaded me to deal with the unresolved emotions that I had for years. At first, it was difficult to pinpoint the cause of the deeply rooted fear that left me feeling rejected and abandoned.

As I continued to share, there was an admission that could not be dismissed or overlooked. There was a childhood memory of my mother I had been too ashamed to admit, but I knew there was no escaping it any longer. I was exposed, and there was no turning back. As I wept, I found the strength to be real - *I didn't love my mother.*

My mother passed away when I was seven years old. Since her death more than forty years ago, I've reflected on what I knew of her, but everything has been seen through the filter of my youth. Memories of her are limited, and there have been numerous times that I've stumbled upon questions that only she would have the answers to. I wanted to ask her if she even loved me. I craved to know if I was planned or if I *just happened*. I sought to tell her the lack of nurturing I suffered left a significant void in my life. If I could somehow find a way to talk to my mother, I would have told her how angry I was that she had abandoned me. My mother's absence conjured up similar feelings when I got divorced, and friendships dissolved, leaving me feeling alone, unloved, and forsaken. I wasn't supposed to grow up without her. It was her that was supposed to be cheering me on from the sidelines of life accomplishments. It was her voice that I should have heard say, "You can do it." Instead, her death stole so many things from our past, present, and future. I needed to reconcile some of the feelings that had been tucked away for so long.

As I struggled to come to grips with the fact that I had finally admitted my feelings about my mother, I found myself face to face with a painful reality that I refused to confront for so long. So, let me put it out there. I had been crippled by the fear of being my most authentic self. I was a people pleaser. I wanted the approval of others, and I didn't want to disappoint any-one. I'd trained myself to act, speak and be exactly who everyone expected. In my eyes, not loving your mother was a fact that was beyond horrible, and it was wrong. I was afraid of my feelings towards her not being un-derstood. I was terrified of being isolated. Surely, I'd be an outcast to my family and friends. They would think differently about me for my candid admission about her. I was scared to deal with my emotions because I thought not sharing them would somehow make it less true and ultimately keep the false narrative alive.

With help, I was able to confront the anxiety asso-ciated with authenticity. While extremely taxing, doing so allowed me to uncover some hard truths. I realized that my lack of candor wasn't about what others thought about me; it was really about what I thought about my-self. I hated myself for not loving my mother. I was em-barrassed, and I felt guilty. I carried the shame for so long that trying to release it was difficult and exhausting. Fac-ing the harsh reality that my fear was based on self-inflict-ed emotions and not my mother's death was frightening.

But not only was I face to face with my dread, I also found myself resting in a safe space that allowed me to make peace with my deepest mindsets. Being genuine wasn't as scary as I had imagined. The people-pleaser mentality I had embraced was gradually replaced with the courage to express myself without apprehension of what others thought.

The pivotal moment in this process was realizing that the little girl with questions and the grown woman who was honest enough to say I didn't love my mother is what authenticity is all about. The path to this type of freedom outweighed the heaviness I carried in living a lie. I was less concerned about the consequence of my integrity because I had been damaged long enough to be dishonest with myself. Finally, I could be me, and others would respect my truth. Showing up as *God is still working on me* has been terrifying sometimes, but it has also been more rewarding than I ever dreamed. The fear of being naked and ashamed was gone, and I refused to apologize for it.

As I progressed through some of my challenges, I didn't realize that God was building me up to serve other women to be their authentic selves. Of course, he was preparing me, but I needed to walk through the process first. If I was going to give my all in this assignment and fully shine the way God intended, I had to faithfully show up, speak my whole truth and embrace the fearfully and wonderfully made woman God created me to be. I've learned that the more genuine and honest I am with myself, the more freedom it gives others in their truth.

I no longer worry that my reality might offend, alienate, or intimidate people. The hiding, playing small, and staying quiet no longer serve me. I have released the old beliefs and lies embedded in me. I've also released the victim mentality and embraced the power to persevere and be present for myself.

Forgiving and loving myself was a major part of overcoming the fear of authenticity. I would sometimes replay my negative thoughts and then punish myself for thinking them. I had to acquire the skills to cultivate kindness, honor, and extend myself grace. I accepted the past and focused on what I could control at the moment. I found the strength and courage to do the necessary inner work to reconnect to my true self. In turn, it allowed my unfiltered realness to radiate through me. It was hard to acknowledge some of my life experiences. Still, once I permitted myself to feel the emotions, it was easier to release my anger. I still have questions for my mother, and I still hold on to my truth about how I feel towards her. However, I am no longer consumed with self-imposed shame.

Authenticity is hard. I carried such sadness that I held onto unhealthy attachments that caused me to react from a place of fear. There were times that I lived inside and outside of the lie. But the fact is, *I am not a liar*, and neither is God. Why? Because He already told me who I was. According to Ephesians 2:10, *I am God's workmanship created to produce good works.* There was a time when the workings of the embedded lies had me in a dark place, but I am now light in the Lord. I am who I am.

The truth of the matter is...

Fear is a natural emotion, but the truth is that it doesn't stand a chance when I place my faith in God, who is stronger and more powerful. There are times that I still struggle with walking in my authenticity, but in those moments, I simply reflect on the last time the truth set me free. Whenever I feel inauthentic, I pray and allow myself to be vulnerable before God and allow His grace to cover those moments of weakness. God doesn't push me away. Instead, He reminds me of how perfectly He made me. Nothing can replace the freedom that I experience as I embrace every facet of me. Being authentic is freeing and beautiful, and it looks good on me.

Joshua 1:9, "*Have I not commanded you? Be strong and courageous*," is a beautiful reminder that I have nothing to fear. The truth is that the fear of authenticity could have permanently paralyzed me. Still, the power within me was far greater than what tried to cripple me. The tears were many, but the fight to become the best version of myself and to confess daily that I am who God says I am, was worth it. I have released the fear component from the equation and embraced the power and freedom that comes with being my authentic self. I no longer fear being the incredible woman God created me to be.

My fear of authenticity allowed me to transform and create a pathway to walk in divine purpose. My transformation is now the inspiration for others and empowers them to walk in their genuineness. My journey has been life-changing, and it is a true testament to what happens when you fight through every adversity. It is a journey that has pushed me to trust God no matter what and to declare that nothing is too hard for Him. I believe that whatever concerns me concerns Him – even my authenticity. This has been a process of self-discovery, self-love, and clarity. I'm glad God chose this path for me and grateful that He gave me the strength to endure. Fear tried to bully me into remaining silent. It was never intended for me to come out from the shadows and be audacious enough to share my story. But the fact is that I conquered my anxiety, and now I shine in my amazing authentic self.

To you, the reader: Being your true self can be very intimidating, yet it's very empowering. Of course, it's risky and sometimes uncomfortable. It carries the weight of being vulnerable and a real fear of rejection. But it's also one of the greatest gifts you can give yourself and offer to others at the same time. It takes bravery to be honest, and in the absence of it, you muzzle your soul's ability to express itself.

This journey to the place of authenticity is a lifetime process. It's a journey that's worth the commitment of liberation. I encourage you to remove the mask and stop conforming to what others think or say. You no longer have to conceal or suppress who you truly are. You matter, and every part of you is valid. Your bona fide self is waiting for you to discover all of who you are without apology and excuses.

Being true to who you are is crucial to building meaningful relationships. It requires words, actions, and behaviors to consistently match your core identity. Brene' Brown describes authenticity this way, "Authenticity is not something we have or don't have. It is a practice – a conscious choice of how we want to live. Authenticity is a collection of choices we have to make every day. It's about the choice to show up and be real. The choice, to be honest. The choice to let our true selves be seen."

When we are in tune with our authentic selves, we become more connected, and our relationships with others are deepened. Trading our authentic selves for the security of being liked or for the approval of others is no longer necessary, and we must trust ourselves to become who we really are. When we are authentic, we exude a genuine confidence that cannot be manufactured.

The Fear of Imperfection

Shannon Nicole

I used to *hate* hearing people say, "Do it afraid." To me, the presence of fear is a surefire sign that something is wrong. I have *religiously* used fear as an indicator to determine whether I should make a move, commit to something or someone, or run like mad! If it is not perfect or I am not *perfect*, it is not meant to be. The only problem with that belief is how I am measuring perfection and, greater still, why that is the gauge.

I grew up as an only child and was not raised in an environment where I felt safe making mistakes. My parents divorced when I was 18-months old but remarried my senior year in high school. So, for 15 years, my mother was the primary authority figure in my life. What she said and thought of me mattered. In elementary school, I struggled a great deal with math and science. I would practice, do homework, mom would help me, and I would go to school and fail tests/ quizzes repeatedly. While helping me with math homework one day, she said to me, "I'm getting you a tutor because this is stupid. I don't understand what you're not getting." I remember at that very moment feeling inadequate. I could understand that she felt frustrated because *she* could not help me, but how was that my fault? I did not know what I did not know. Though she did get me a tutor, I still struggled. I seemed to understand when the tutor was with me but could not reproduce it when I went back into the classroom. Furthermore, I was ashamed to ask for help because I thought I was *supposed* to already know what I did not know and had already asked for help but still got it wrong.

Over time, the internal pressure to be perfect became an obsession. I trained myself to wait for all conditions to be favorable before I attempted tasks. I needed situations to be ideal. If they weren't, I ran or hid. But, of course, perfection never really happens. I lived under a constant sense of rejection; I didn't feel good enough, worthy enough, and nothing I did seemed to be enough. So, I strove for perfection because the consequences of imperfection far outweighed the benefits of trying. I had to have (and get) the absolute correct right answers, so I would frequently rehearse conversations and reactions over and over – ones I expected to have and ones I had in the past. It was tiring.

Worst yet, when a situation would arise that I prepped for and I did not respond the way I projected, I fell into condemnation. I would think, *Why can I always think of the right thing to say or do after the moment has passed? Why did this not come to me when it counted?* It was important to me to make the best decisions, but I did nothing if I felt undecided. Inaction was my go-to for the uncomfortable or scary. I aspired to have *perfect* knowledge of everything. If I did not know it all, I would not attempt to start; there was no such thing as on-the-job training because I did not want to risk getting it wrong. Doing so meant there was something wrong with *me*. I had so much pride, and I stubbornly reverted to self-preservation to protect myself from any discomfort.

Because I felt so insecure, I would write notes and letters to express myself in a conversation with people who were more outspoken, confident, or could possibly reject me. To this day, I still do this; I prefer it over face-to-face conversations. Some may say it's hiding behind the text; to me, it's avoiding an uncomfortable conversation with outcomes I cannot control. I began the note-and-letter-writing expressly with my mother when I was a teenager because when we talked, I would try to share my thoughts and feelings but would leave the conversations feeling unheard (because she often talked over me), misunderstood (because my thoughts seemed to become jumbled and I would not be able to effectively convey them), and dejected (because I never met my mother's communication expectations). If I disagreed with her, she would get angry. So, I figured I could sort through what I wrote with her in conversation if I could just get it out. Well, my mother despised my notes. There were times that she would read them and then tear them up in front of me, stating that I only wrote them because I did not want to hear what she had to say. But nothing could be further than the truth; I just wanted to feel accepted even if she did not agree.

I also struggled with finishing. I dropped out of college multiple times; what should've taken four years took me ten and $75,000+ in student loan debt. I was double-minded and unsure about many things. I longed for approval and affirmation and thought the only way I could get it was if I did everything *just right*. That is when my self-sabotage began. If I failed a test, I dropped a class. If I made good grades, I overcompensated and spun myself into a web of attempting to overachieve, even if that meant I had to compromise or lie to do it. Once in college, I had a research paper due, one in which I procrastinated to begin. I pulled an all-night-er, taking short sleeping breaks because it was due the following morning at the close of my professor's office hours. I did not finish in time and frantically contacted him, stating I had printing issues and was on my way to campus. I lied. I did not want to face the consequence of missing a deadline or failing a class. I did the work. I passed the class. I scored well on the paper. But it damaged my *perfect* image because I knew I was not honest.

I was obsessed with the idea of one right move, which couldn't be discerned if there were no steps taken. I hated consequences – after all, they wouldn't be necessary if I was *perfect*. As a result, I lived indecisive, double-minded, and depressed. I would make a decision and renege or start projects and not see them through. Instead of embracing the fear and moving in the right direction, I panicked. I also could not bear seeing the flaws in my character; I felt like I had no control over them and did not know how to change them. After all, I *tried* before and kept failing.

What's more? I was constantly compared to others. When I didn't complete college as expected, and one of my cousins did, I was met with disapproval yet again. I was *supposed* to be a speech pathologist but dropped out. I *should have* finished but did not. "That should be you graduating. I am so disappointed in you!" This comment reiterated what I already believed. This belief system influenced every other thought about me: I was not good enough. I was *imperfect*. The idea of *good enough* produced a people-pleasing habit in me. I yearned for approval but, ironically, did not like people depending on me. I feared messing up and failing them. Performance pressure made me cower at moments that really mattered, like completing college.

During my 10-year undergraduate career at Old Dominion University, I decided to major in communication and journalism. I figured I could analyze what I was doing wrong in a neutral environment. I wanted so badly to just enjoy communicating and feeling safe in it. I enjoyed the in-class conversations and learning the science of communication. However, writing (not speaking) had become highly cathartic for me. It was the one thing I felt I did very well, even if I was the only one reading what I wrote. When it was time to share my writing with the public, I was apprehensive about letting others read it for fear of harsh critique. In my Advanced Composition Literature class, one of the assignments was writing a memoir and using creative language to help my readers see, hear, feel, smell, and taste what I experienced. I wrote about my first car accident, in which I totaled the car I received as a high school graduation gift. What was interesting to me was how long it took me to decide what to write. I did not know what I wanted to remember, much less share. Once I decided, I had the details in my head but could not put anything on paper. I kept rehearsing what I would write, afraid the outcome would not meet expectations and how I would respond.

So, there I was, knowing that I knew *how* to write but was paralyzed by the fear of imperfection. Is this story good enough? Then, finally, my teacher, Professor Julie Manthey, disrupted my spiraling thoughts with an email message:

Shannon,

I hope that you are indeed finally coming to the realization that what you have to share through your writing is always worthy -- for any audience. And yes, the best writers have the best editors -- never forget that. You are a gifted writer, Shannon, but you can't share that gift until you actually put it down on paper. I know in your heart of hearts you know this -- you must not allow your insecurities to deter you from your writing – ever. I will always support you, help you, or give you a swift quick in the behind – whatever the need is at the time. Have a wonderful holiday weekend, and I'll see you in class.

Julie

Her words were the seeds I needed planted to become confident as a writer. Reading someone believed in me and would be willing to coach me through assignments meant the world to me. After graduating from college in 2008, I occupied several different jobs but always had this knack for writing. Even in my notes and letters to friends, I frequently heard, "Shannon, you always seem to know just what to say." From my experiences, I believe God birthed a desire to encourage others through writing. It took nine years and seven months, but, as of December 2016, I am now the author of two published works, an active blogger, and, of course, a co-author in the anthology you are holding in your hands. If I had waited to be *perfect*, I would still be waiting today. Whenever I question the value of what I have to say or write, I remind myself of this Scripture that has been used to define and support my calling in this world: *The Sovereign Lord has given me his words of wisdom so that I know how to comfort the weary. Morning by morning, he wakens me and opens my understanding to his will* (Isaiah 50:4, New Living Translation).

I think it is not strange that the very things God gives to strengthen and encourage others using my words are the very things the enemy uses to buffet and attempt to seduce me into silence. Words come into our ears, but we have the choice of allowing them to enter our hearts.

The truth of the matter is . . .

I am *not* perfect, but God does not require me to be. I admit I still struggle with this truth and am extremely hard on myself when I make genuine mistakes. However, I remind myself that my flaws are not automatic disqualifiers; they are opportunities for my growth and character development. For example, the same girl with a learning deficiency in math became an elementary school teacher *teaching math*. It took me six years of teaching to dismantle the lie that I was not good enough or needed to know it all to be effective. In 2020, God placed me on a high-performing teaching team among people who never looked down on me for what I did not know. When I made mistakes or did not understand something, they were there to help me no matter how embarrassed I felt. They took their time and taught me, and I listened and learned. I lost the intimidation of math and gained an appreciation for learning strategies I use to help students who struggled in math as I had as a child. I finished the last school year with a highly effective teacher evaluation. I had to embrace a new mindset that perfection was not required; humility was.

Another truth. . .

My mom didn't think I was stupid when she tried to help me with my homework. She was a single parent, dealing with her own issues and pressures. My mother was managing her emotions and my needs, which I can imagine was challenging. She had a moment of frustration. She loved me, or she would not have gotten me help. Her devotion was evident in her provision, sacrifices, and support. In fact, when I brought home a D in math on a report card, my mom said she rejoiced because the D looked like an A to her; she knew how hard I struggled and was just happy it was not an F. That does not sound like perfection was required of me. As a mom myself, I am learning not to impose undue pressure on my middle-school-aged daughter to perform. Perfection is not required of her, just obedience and an honest effort.

My final truth. . .

I am NOT God! I realized I depended too much on my ability, comfort, and the idol of perfectionism which made me miss out on defining moments in my faith walk. To insist on my way, ideals, and comfort is to deny God's plan for my life, and I no longer want to participate in that lifestyle. Not every situation will seem favorable, but my appropriate response to God in those moments is the difference between reward and regret. He has already factored in the unknowns, and unwavering faith in Him is required to navigate those. So, I have to quiet the fear with obedience - every time. Selective obedience does not conquer fear. I understand fully that my flesh will *never* want to obey, so I cannot function in my own strength because I am going to fail God and me every time. I must depend on the only *perfect* One who would never ask me to do anything He has not given me the power to do.

The Fear of Exposure

Mavis Rowe, LCSW

"I hate it here!" These were the words I wrote in an email to my book coach when I agreed to participate in this project. I was overwhelmed with my life and still am in many regards. I like being shrouded in obscurity in my introverted corner because it's where I've been most of my life and where I'm most comfortable. However, God is pushing me out of my comfort zone like a baby bird evicted from its nest, and it scares me beyond rational thought. As a social worker and in ministry, professions that require human exchanges of openness, intelligence, compassion, and faith, I know I had to first acknowledge the conflict to begin the healing process. Then, identify the vice and speak the truth about that thing. So here it goes.

Hello, my name is Mavis, and I struggle with the fear of exposure, and my vice is the fear of being on exhibition for the world to see.

This sounds like my first confessional in a 12-step program, and in a way, it is. Professionals refer to it as the fear of success (achievemephobia), and some call it the fear of being seen (scoptophobia). In my case, it is a little of both with an unhealthy dose of self-doubt mixed in for good measure. I am scared of my intellect and abilities being observed by strangers and those I have yet to allow within my inner circle. I'm anxious about the praise or validation I may receive because I probably won't measure up to the expectations of my supporters. I accept others' accolades about my work with trepidation because they are inconsistent with my family members' feedback growing up. Praise is uncomfortable because it makes me feel like an imposter. These strong beliefs have roots in my childhood, and it's that emotional trauma that continues to steal my joy and cripple my progress.

I was reared in an environment where negative critiques were used as a response to my failures in the great hope of encouraging my success. My mother was adamant that I be *the best* academically. (A)s were the expectation, but I received no praise when I met her demands; however, I received a lot of negative attention when I was academically insufficient. I felt I had no choice but to excel in pleasing my mom, which caused tension in my other relationships. My siblings sought to use negative comments to teach me that I was less than ordinary and box me into their levels of achievement. At school, I was a nerd by society's standards. I was not popular and was recognized as one of the geeky kids. I was smart, but I dared not share this with peers outside of my honors and advanced placement classes because it would allow them to continue my social torture. My response to it all was to function at the upper echelon of my class but conceal the fact from everyone around me except my mother, who expected greatness. Though I was in advanced courses, I never shared my grades, cultivated no authentic friendships, and shied away from social events. I was protecting myself. I progressed in the dark while secretly wishing for acceptance. When it didn't come, I withdrew into myself, refusing to allow anyone to see the real me.

After high school and before entering college, I began to absorb my cover. I believed it was better to exist in the shadows and be unnoticeable. I didn't share my opinions or expertise even when I knew I could be helpful. I convinced myself that I was a fraud and didn't possess the skills to assist in any situation. My insecurities had me questioning the validity of the strength of my voice in this world, and I doubted anyone cared about what I had to say. Yes, I knew I was smart and could impact others, but I was afraid I was lying to myself and living in a deluded reality. I thought that anyone could do what I was doing, so my efforts were no big deal and should not be celebrated. I bought into the narrative that I was insignificant, and eventually, it became a part of my identity. I was convinced that I was not special, and my success would never be appreciated by others or would incite anger among those who lacked my gifts, so I kept quiet about everything.

As I began my freshman year in college, I encountered a peer who had me questioning my behaviors but not enough to make me want to change them. I was a non-traditional student with a family and responsibilities, and we had a major history exam. It had 50 questions, and half the test was essay-style. The week after the exam, we received our grades, and one of the younger male students asked me my score. I gave a vague response, but he wouldn't let it go. Finally, he pressed, and I caved, disclosing a perfect score of 136, which included 36 extra credit points. He gave me this odd look and told me that I should never play small for anyone and that I should be proud of my grade, shout it from the risers even. I thought he was funny, but his words were a crack in my reclusive shell. It was the first time I explored being more visible and transparent. I didn't change my coping style of concealment, but I began to think about the lie that I chose to believe.

I eventually became a clinical social worker and accepted a call to ministry. Still, I wanted to remain enveloped in my impenetrable veil. Working with others in an intimate setting was acceptable for this introvert. However, speaking to authority figures about my prowess increased my anxiety tenfold. I shied away from public speaking events, group sessions, seminars, or any area where I may have to reveal myself. I became a pro at dodging the public eye until God required more from me and intentionally placed me in situations that required me to share my talents with large groups. From work-related mental health training to facilitating wellness groups on social media platforms, I had to educate without being reserved before large groups of people. It was no longer advantageous to my destiny to remain isolated. The more I resisted, the more anxiety consumed me. I started to become physically sick when the thought of exposure loomed. It began to affect my work, church, and home life as public assignments continued to pile on my plate.

I remember the first time I had to talk before the congregation at my church. I worked at a behavioral center and participated in the annual *Out of Darkness Walk,* a fundraising event to bring awareness to suicide and depression. My pastor asked me to talk to the congregation about attending the walk and facilitating mental health training per the church's insurance policy. My knee-jerk reaction was to say no, but I knew I could not deny his request. I was the only professional in the congregation who could manage the task, and I reluctantly acquiesced. The morning I was to speak, nervousness settled on me like a cloak of darkness. My speech was eight minutes long, but it felt like I had walked the green mile.

When it was my time to speak, I got up from my comfortable back row seat on the unsaved side of the church; the name was affectionately given to the section farthest away from the pulpit. My legs were weak, my heart was palpitating, and my hands stiffened. I stood before the attendees, and I swear it felt like everyone in the city had come to see me choke. As I spoke, my voice was shaky and sounded like I was on the brink of tears with my labored breathing. I assumed the congregation thought nothing was amiss because I had just shared that I had lost a co-worker to suicide one week earlier. It appeared that I was overcome with grief, but in actuality, my current state had nothing to do with that loss of life. Instead, I was in a full-blown panic and succumbed to the torture of being seen by this group of people for the first time. Before this, they knew almost nothing about me because I had blended into the background on that back pew. I wasn't clamoring to be in the choir, on the usher board, or the children's ministry. I was a missionary but only after having my arm twisted by a family member. Because I was quiet, it came as a shock to many when I stood up to speak that Sunday.

I eventually made it through my speech and went back to my seat. The pastor was giving the benediction, and I was just beginning to breathe normally and get my body back under control, but that comfort was short-lived. As I looked around, there were eyes on me. At first, I thought it was in my mind, but when people began to approach me after service, I realized that I had just been outed and instantly wanted to run away. However, my escape was thwarted by questions from the crowd, a crowd I should have been comfortable with because many were family and others were people I have known since marrying my husband. Because this fear of exposure is about more than normal social anxiety, my familiarity with the crowd was inconsequential. They asked me questions like, "What do you do for a living again?" or "Can you be on this board or that board?" They also made statements like, "Girl, you sure surprised me!" or "I didn't know you were smart." By the end of the day, I was experiencing an emotional overload. The need to get away became as vital as breathing. I felt raw, vulnerable, and exposed to the harsh reality of expected public scrutiny and criticism. It was too much. I liken it to Jesus, in the book of John, being told by his mother to turn water into wine at the wedding in Cana. He told her his "hour had not come yet." So likewise, I felt that my exposure was premature. It wasn't time. It was too scary, and I preferred to stay in the shadows, but God had another plan.

It was time to come out of the darkness of my self-imposed seclusion and stop believing the lie. And I did just that. To say my life got busy is an understatement, but somehow, I've managed to survive it all. If I had to share all the ways God has exposed me since that Sunday, I would need another chapter, and we don't have time for that. I will share, however, what is going on now to give some perspective. As I pen this, I am in the middle of publishing my first book on grief. I'm a geriatric therapist and must duel with insurance companies who challenge my authority when dealing with workplace chaos. I'm transforming from a parent to a consultant with the adult humans I have birthed and continue to prioritize cultivating a healthy marriage. I am also becoming more visible at my church and have been given new duties that will push me further into the spotlight. No more hiding or being hero support by helping others be great. Whew! This alone can be traumatic and consuming for an introvert who prefers invisibility. But wait. There's more. To add to all of this, God says, "Oh, do all of that while in seminary with papers, group projects, sermons, and lectures upon lectures," in addition to maneuvering through the disordered university administrative processes amid COVID-19. I feel like I'm white-knuckling trying to hold on to my seemingly unremarkable life, but the Creator Tornado, aka God, is snatching my hands away so I can latch onto purpose.

The truth of the matter is...

I don't like it here, but God will not allow me to remain in my shelter of comfort. Somebody out there needs to see me! I realize that it's not the discomfort of the swirling activity that bothers me; it's the fear of being audacious and having my intelligence illuminated that is causing me great trepidation. When I am in my private space, others won't know how amazing I am; then, I will not have to show up. God is telling me it's time to reveal myself, and I want to run for cover, but that too has been seized. So, what do I do? I have no choice but to set my anxiety aside and let purpose guide me to my destination.

Another truth is that I'm worried that I may be an imposter and that others will harshly scrutinize things I value about my character. Most of all, I am terrified that I will not recognize this new person, this new me. The unassuming girl of my past is someone I had an intimate relationship with. Now I am bold and purpose-driven, and it's intimidating at times. How do I get to know, understand, and protect the new me? I'm on display for all to see, and there are no protective shields except the knowledge that I have value and the favor of God. Yet, I am strong and unafraid to lend my voice to the world. I love myself fiercely and won't allow others to diminish my sparkle. The lie is shattered every time I walk to a podium or a pulpit because I know I have a voice that needs to be heard.

Am I still afraid? Yes, but I won't allow the lies to thrive. Letting it take root again will derail my destiny. I will not allow this to happen because I am a role model for my children and others who gain inspiration from my success. We go through things, not for us, but for others to provide them with hope and encouragement. I can't let us down, and most importantly, I won't let God down. I will feel the fear and do it anyway because I know my destiny is waiting.

The Fear of Judgment

Dr. Angela Corprew-Boyd

"Therefore, let us stop passing judgment on one another. Instead, make up your mind not to put any stumbling block or obstacle in the way of a brother or sister" (Romans 14:13, NIV).

As a little girl, I dreamt of becoming a tv reporter. I'd stand in front of the television holding a spoon or broom handle as a microphone and recited the local news anchor's cadence and tone verbatim. As I grew into a teenager, I held on to my aspiring profession, but it was challenging to do. I had chosen mentors as role models, but their voices echoed scathing criticism, and they spoke to me out of ignorance and cultural proclivity. I would hear comments such as, "You should not talk so proper, or you don't have to talk like a white person." Over time, I got tired of hearing from people I respected using such derogatory words. As a young adult, I was taught to listen to the wisdom of others, but they could not see my growth; I was still a child in their eyes in which children were seen and not heard. This led me to wonder if they knew their words were a stumbling block in my belief in becoming a television news reporter. Although I respected them as people, I concluded, they did not know who God had created me to be. And because I did not know, "I was fearfully and wonderfully made," I allowed the fear of judgment (opinions and pain striking words) to destroy what God had predestined for my life.

Years later, I attended college and majored in what I considered my second nature, Mass Communications. It was not often you would see or hear about black women news reporters, so I would be amongst the first and few. I was practicing my craft and evolving as a young woman at the same time. I spoke proper grammar, pronouncing and carefully enunciating my words correctly. In front of the camera, I wanted to be the best when the time arrived. I was on my way to realizing my dream until going home and reconnecting with family, friends, and role models who shared with me a different outlook on my career choice. For some reason, I was "too good or proper" for the culture I so readily accepted all my life. It did not matter that some family had broken English and even spoke Ebonics. Who really cared? I just wanted to be accepted because of the person I was grooming myself to be. I did not seem good enough to them because I was evolving into someone else. I would hear, "You do not have to speak like those people or speak so proper." I became so frustrated and felt bullied and badgered that I made fewer trips home; I began to doubt if I had chosen the right career.

I was getting no encouragement because the ones I respected could not see me as a young black woman on a television screen. I remedied this and was able to please myself at the same time. So, I dummied down who I was and reverted to who they expected when I went home on a visit. At school, I continued practicing my craft and speaking proper English. It was difficult to be two different people. Eventually, the masquerade ended with me losing. I could not manage the pretense any longer. Their judgment became discouragement which transformed to disappointment, and disappointment became despair. That was a brutal blow to my self-esteem, which swallowed my confidence. I felt failure had overcome me. After two successful years in the program, I gave up on my dream job and chose a different direction (education). My credible others did not see the plans God had for me, and truth be told, I no longer saw them either. This took me to a dark place.

I cried and waddled in fear of judgment for months. This unfortunate state paralyzed me to keep my mouth shut, and I did. I chose not to discuss the pain I felt and kept it to myself. I repeatedly replayed the tapes of criticism and judgment in my mind, which kept my struggle fresh and made it difficult to release. The more I embraced defeat, the more critical I was of myself. But one day, God sent me an angel in the form of my English instructor at Virginia State University. She read a paper I had written for an assignment in her class. The title was "Don't Judge Me!" I shared bits and pieces of my story within it, not imagining she would realize I was the main character. This opened the door for dialogue and a pathway to my healing. I will never forget her words when I asked, "How do you deal with yourself when you have held your credible others' words as honorable, and they were the cause of shifting your career before it began?" She responded with four simple words, "You must be willing." Of course, my next question was, "Willing to do what?"

I had several writing assignments to complete in the subsequent weeks for Ms. Harding. Throughout the themes of my papers were judgment, fear, and emotional pain. On my last assignment, she wrote a note on my paper, "See me, 10:00 am," and her phone number. I was reluctant to go because I didn't know what to expect. When I arrived in her office, I sat down and began to sob uncontrollably with my face covered by my hands. Immediately I felt a tender hand on my back, and I heard a still small voice say, "Are you willing?" It was at that point I lifted my head, and there was such a peace in her office that my lips moved and said, "Yes." I saw her reaching on a bookshelf above my head, and she pulled down her Bible. She read, "He sent his word, and healed them, and delivered them from their own destructions" (Psalm 107:20, KJV). She gazed into my eyes and said, "You were on the road to destruction, but God sent an angel to save you." Again, I cried and pleaded through my tears for God to help me, and He did.

Ms. Harding picked me up from my dorm for church every Sunday for the next few months. Her Pastor was preaching on ways to stop living in fear of judgment and learning how to free yourself to be yourself. Wow! God really did send an angel to save me. However, before I could say, "I am willing," I had to realize fear had debilitated me because I allowed it. My thoughts were not focused on wholesome things that would bring glory to God or things that would catapult me out of my misery into my destiny. I had a choice, but I could not

pull my mind from thinking someone had taken something away from me, and I let them do it. I resented the
judgments and those who hurled them at me. I did not
want to forgive them because they did not deserve to be
forgiven to me. Finally, the Spirit of the Lord arrested
me with the scripture, "Repay no one evil for evil but
give thought to do what is honorable in the sight of all"
(Romans 12:17, ESV). Thank God for my desperation
because it had ignited a fire within me that I needed. I
no longer wanted to stay in a debilitative condition because I was *willing* to forgive and move forward. I said,
"I'm willing," and I was able to be delivered.

The points in his messages brought me out of my
dark place and took me on a journey of self-worth.
Week after week, I felt my pain dissolving and the
weight of judgment lifting from my spirit, and it was
because *I was willing*. There were many points to his
message, but the following are the ones I remember
most because I put them into practice; they were critical to my deliverance:

1. **Do not accept judgment:** "Therefore, there is
    now no condemnation for those who are in Christ
    Jesus, because through Christ Jesus the law of the
    Spirit who gives life has set you free from the law
    of sin and death" (Romans 8:1-2, NIV).

2. **Do not internalize critical thoughts:** "Finally, brothers and sisters, whatever is true, whatever is noble, whatever is right, whatever is pure, whatever is lovely, whatever is admirable—if anything is excellent or praiseworthy—think about such things (Philippians 4:8).

3. **Do not seek approval from others:** "For am I now seeking the approval of man, or of God? Or am I trying to please man? If I were still trying to please man, I would not be a servant of Christ" (Galatians 1:10, ESV).

4. **Do not judge but love yourself:** "And he answered saying, 'Thou shalt love the Lord thy God with all thy heart, and with all thy soul, and with all thy strength, and with all thy mind; and thy neighbor as thyself'" (Luke 10:27, KJV).

5. **Do not fear when people judge you:** "For God has not given us a spirit of fear but of power and of love and of a sound mind" (2 Timothy 1:7, KJV).

6. **Forgiveness frees you from your judges:** "For if you forgive other people when they sin against you, your heavenly Father will also forgive you" (Matthew 6:14, NLT).

When I read James 1:22-25, NIV, it propelled me to action. It declares, *"But be doers of the Word, and not hearers only, deceiving yourselves. For if anyone is a hearer of the Word and not a doer, he is like a man observing his natural face in the mirror; for he observes himself, goes away, and immediately forgets what kind of man he was. But he who looks into the perfect law of liberty and continues in it and is not a forgetful hearer but a doer of the work, this one will be blessed in what he does."* So, I decided I wanted to be blessed and live a life of freedom from the judgment of others and myself.

The truth of the matter is...

I allowed credible voices to take precedence over God's Word. Those words were strongholds (anything that exalts itself above the Word of God), and the Bible says, "For the weapons of our warfare are not carnal, but mighty through God to the pulling down of strongholds;" (2 Corinthians 10:4, KJV). Those strongholds distracted, detoured, derailed, and detached me from my desire to be a television news reporter. All because I will admit, I did not know God's Word and what His Word said explicitly about me. But now that I do, the truth is I not only became an online news reporter, but I have my own talk show. I believe God took my dream and deferred it because He wanted to expand it, so my elevation was inevitable when I ultimately released the fear of judgment.

If you are ready and willing, may I suggest you begin to internalize the points I referenced above and allow the scriptures to speak to your spirit. Play them repeatedly in your mind and develop a strategy to move from where you are to the place of peace and freedom you desire. Also, add to your collection of downloads, repeating who the scriptures say you are in Christ. Trust me, the words of God will contradict the judgmental opinions others have expressed about you. This agony from fear of judgment is not an easy and immediate fix; it will take planning, praying, fasting, and forgiving, but it can be done. Activate your plan and put it into action. Develop a daily or weekly routine and stick to it. Distractions may try to interrupt your plan. Judgmental thoughts may try to discourage you from praying. Failure may try to prevent you from fasting. Unforgiveness may try to halt you from forgiving. However, it shall be done. But you must put the work in to see results.

In life, when God entrusts us with a dream, it is not others' purpose to make it come to fruition. I missed that because I was seeking approval from people. I realize now that God is the originator of our desire; "He knew us before he formed us in the womb" (Jeremiah 1:5a, KJV). I now understand I was predestined to be a news reporter. I had already been approved, but I allowed the echoes of others to deter and detour me because I had no idea that God would give me the desires of my heart. The Word declares in Isaiah 55:8-9 (NIV), "For my thoughts are not your thoughts, neither are your ways my ways, declares the Lord. As the heavens are higher than the earth, so are my ways higher than your ways and my thoughts than your thoughts." God informs us that He is obligated to make good on what He has given us. It is bigger (higher) than us. We should not allow other voices to strip us from our dreams. I let the voices of others talk me out of my blessing by receiving their judgment. If I had known to tune in to what God wanted for me, I would have conquered those voices of judgmental people a long time ago. Moreover, I would have understood John 16:33 (KJV), "These things I have spoken unto you, that in me ye might have peace. In the world ye shall have tribulation: but be of good cheer; I have overcome the world."

Now, I seek God to confirm what he has for me and a strategic plan to reach it. Those voices of judgment no longer have the influence to deter or delay my dreams because I know God and who I am! Psalm 34:4, KJV declares, "I sought the Lord, and he answered me: he delivered me from my fears."

The Fear of Disappointing God

Monique Jewell Anderson

My daddy was my biggest cheerleader. He wouldn't let me settle, give excuses, and required greatness from me. I recall as a little girl running on the track with him, and when we approached the finished line, he'd shout, "Always go further than what you said you would." So instead of stopping at the finished line, a goal someone else had set, I ran as far as I could pass it, then I'd turn to see him with a full smile, crooked teeth, and all. When I played left field in softball, daddy would stand by the fence and tell me, "Move up. The ball's coming fast; throw it to first." And when that big girl slid into my leg, and I had to go to the ER, daddy was there handing me his toothpick to bite down on. When I had my son, daddy was there holding my hand. I had promised him years earlier that if I had a son, I would name him Robert too. My father was proud of me, and it was important that he always stayed proud. It was my intent that when people knew I was his daughter, I represented him well. As a US Navy sailor for over 20 years, Robert Jewell was big on family, being timely, consistent, truthful, and hardworking; the tenets of my life. I was a Jewell, not just in last name only – I was valuable, rare, and had to shine. As his days came to a close, daddy was in the hospital; right before he stopped talking for good, he said verbatim, "Monique, you are amazing."

Life got a lot quieter for me when my father died. My once busy calendar of doctor visits, testing, and chemo appointments was also gone. But God and me were cool. I mean, I wasn't mad at Him; instead, I depended on Him, even more, to help heal the void I had in my heart. Daddy had suffered in pain for years, and to know that was over, gave me comfort. But, make no mistake about it, daddy's physical absence, the silence of his silky-smooth voice, was deafening. I was hurt! So, I took some time from the bulk of my ministry duties to get myself together. I hadn't realized the magnitude of grief I would endure until I was uncontrollably in tears, face down on the carpet, unable to physically get up. The effects of his death were palatable in every area of my existence. My daily prayer and confession were Psalms 147:3, "He heals the brokenhearted and binds up their wounds."

I remember the date well. It was the morning of Pentecost Sunday. I woke up excited more than I had in a very long time. It felt good to feel like life had a purpose again. So, when I walked into the prayer room, I just knew something exciting was about to happen. We gathered in a circle, and along with a few others, I, too, was asked to pray, so I did. I walked in my authority and in my anointing like I knew and was trained to do so. I have the gift of healing, so under the guidance of Holy Spirit, I asked if anyone was in need. Like so many times before at other meetings, those in need got into a line, and one by one, I prayed and laid hands. I felt glory release from me. It wasn't an emotion, but more of a force is the best way to describe it. As I paused to pray for another, I saw upper leadership standing in the back, staring at me in a way I had never seen before. I don't know why but my stomach dropped. For a brief second, I felt like a kid about to get in trouble. I brushed the feeling off because I know I don't play with God, His people, or His things. Period. I just want to be found faithful. Anyhow, we wrapped up the prayer moment and entered the sanctuary for corporate worship as usual.

A few days later, and in shock, I was sitting at a round table in front of leadership being reprimanded.

I was told there was a specific assignment to pray for someone else, but my actions were a distraction that prevented that from happening. I was always one to accept the consequences because I was again raised not to give excuses; I verbally apologized. Furthermore, I was told to write a paper on the spirit of Jezebel, which was really strange and straight out of left field. I had no clue what Jezebel had to do with me and my proven character and integrity. Even though I was confused, I submitted to the reprimand and did it, and I still have a copy of it.

To say that I felt terrible doesn't even come close. I was deeply grieved, and my tears just didn't flow from my eyes that day – they flowed from my spirit. I had spent the last five years of my life diligently serving, praying, and interceding for people. There was no way I would ever deliberately prevent an assignment from happening. I was on the wall – faithful, consistent, and fervent as a leader. Thinking the meeting was over, I was asked to stay after the others left. Face to face, my direct leadership said, in essence, I had disappointed God, I couldn't be trusted, and that I was trying to take over their ministry. Me? Did someone else come in the room because they couldn't be describing me? Naw, they got the wrong one. And while I've never been physically stabbed, at that moment, I was spiritually. I wasn't just wounded; it was a blow designed to kill me. In the months and years that followed, I saw the ones I was once in spiritual trenches with pick up a shovel and throw dirt on me. In each one, I saw their eyes dart and their heads turn. I noticed how I received fewer and fewer assignments. The tight hugs and the robust laughs all ceased. The daily calls went silent. It had become painfully official; I was shunned and slowly forced out of a ministry arm that I knew I was called to.

I have many attributes, but phony will never be one of them. I am a straight shooter, and I try hard to keep my heart pure, but this thing, I can honestly say, took me all the way out. I didn't know how to serve God in this new forced capacity of ostracization. And the people I would typically confide in, lean on, left me to fall. The ones I trusted no longer trusted me.

I was isolated in an entire room with those who were trained to heal the bleeding of others and yet, offered me no help and no reprieve. Redemption was for sinners, but not for me. Like an eight-legged spider with venom, the lies were injected and, on constant replay, solidifying their place in my heart and soul, slowly and surely I heard...

You're not anointed.

You can't be trusted.

You have a hidden agenda.

You didn't hear from God.

You listened to the enemy.

You are not a good friend.

Your works are not good enough.

Your sacrifices mean nothing.

Your daddy would be so disappointed in you.

And somewhere between that event and now, even though I've not talked about it nor tried to persuade anyone to the contrary, I spiritually believed the lies. The confidence in my ability to hear anything (good) from God took a significant hit. I retreated to the only place I felt safe…in isolation and silence. I stopped talking. I stopped praying. Again, it wasn't abrupt but subtle. However, when I looked in the mirror, I knew a part of Monique had died too, not just my daddy. Not one to be a people pleaser, it was (and still is) my desire to please God, and the thought of me potentially not doing that wrecked me. There was a connection; physically, my earthly father was gone, and spiritually so was my relationship with my heavenly father.

I had a dilemma; to do what I was called to do (pray and intercede), I'd have to do so besides those who chose to believe the worst of me without the benefit of at least asking me the truth.

The truth of the matter is simple; I was wrong.

Truth #1: I have never liked getting in trouble - not as a child and surely not as an adult. Somewhere along the way, I have equated trouble, failure, or mistakes as inferior, less than. Maybe it's perfectionism; I can be overly critical of myself mainly because I like to represent my heavenly Father well. When He looks at me, I want, no, I need Him to be proud of me – just like my daddy was. So, I'm learning to receive and extend grace to myself just as I do to others. This is my first time living, and clearly, I won't always get it right, but I will keep trying.

Truth #2. I mismanaged relationships. I unconsciously placed leadership on a throne they didn't die for. I held their opinions in great regard and allowed their influence to be larger than the truth. As a result, my willingness to serve got misconstrued as a servant. I don't do the blame game thing, I'm too mature for that, plus it's pointless. This is my life, and I'm solely responsible for it.

Truth #3: My biggest regret was staying silent. It made me look weak and guilty, and I hated that.

I should have spoken up for myself. Not to confront or cause confusion but to gain clarity and closure. My voice is my power and my saving grace. My voice has opened so many doors that otherwise would have remained shut. I know when I speak, situations change, yet I kept my mouth shut. Matthew 12:34, "Out of the abundance of the heart, the mouth speaks." My heart had grown cold and silent – which affected my mouth. My ability and willingness to pray, praise, worship, and trust – was gone. I had convinced myself I had disappointed God to the point that He didn't want to hear from me. This belief took root down in my soul.

However, the reality, the truth, was so much closer than the lies. *God never told me I disappointed him – ever!*

While I may have failed man in their expectation of me that day, who I am at my core will never disappoint God. Oh, I am well aware and remind God often all about me and my flaws, yet he still smiles at me when I'm in His presence. I am His creation – not an oops, I didn't mean to make Monique. God created me with specificity in mind. He knew he had to make me strong so I would have the strength to hold my head up above the fray. I had to resist the urge to get even, to tell *my side,* and instead allow God to fight on my behalf the way He wanted to. And frankly, I had to open my dog-on heart! I forced myself to love my enemies.

Truth #4: I disappointed myself. I knew better to believe man over God, yet it happened. Anyone can be manipulated given the right time and situation. After everyone left the room, those hurtful and manipulative words spoken to me in private really revealed their issue and insecurities – not mine. Those words should have hit the floor and stayed right there. But instead, I carried them in my heart and memories everywhere I went. I felt displaced and insignificant. I second and tripled guessed my calling and anointing and often chose not to operate in either of them. Painful but true: I disqualified myself. As much as I hated the pain, I still decided to embrace it. It's bad enough to fall but choosing to stay down is a whole nother kind of unnecessary punishment. I had to get a grip before I ended up dead and full of potential.

Truth #5: The fear of disappointing God allowed me to recognize self-made idols. I had to prioritize and place people in their perspective places, allowing me to move forward. But first, I had to repent. I let a once credible authority alter the plans God had for me. Their words had clearly unearthed an ungodly belief I had buried about myself. I had to tear that idol down, and I had to renew my thoughts and my faith in God. Not to get too churchy, but I had to cast down every vain imagination that tried to rise above the Word of God concerning my life. I learned to believe in myself again and to laugh at my doubters and haters. As a result, God opened some prominent doors for me that I believe would have never opened had I remained tethered and yoked to a destiny other than my own. I know He did it because I weathered the storm. I did not blow my witness because, at the end of the day, that's all I have. I kept my mouth shut concerning others. I celebrated even when I didn't have to. I guarded my heart and constantly prayed Psalms 51:10, "Create in me a clean heart, o God. Renew a right spirit within me."

Deliverance from the fear of disappointing God meant that God's truth and my truth had to be aligned and on the same page. I know what I did and what I didn't do. But, if the lies remain, and they do, I still had choices to make. The words God has spoken and promised me had to be enough. They had to be, and ultimately, they were.

The last and most important truth: God loves me, all of Monique. His plans for me have not changed, nor will they ever. Even when I didn't believe in myself and still questioned my call, God strategically placed credible witnesses around me to confirm what HE said about me. They loved on me and held my hand until I got steady enough to walk on my own again. They saw me! I will forever be grateful to God for divine relationships.

Words are powerful! Use them wisely, soberly, and in love.

Fear of The Finish Line

Marcia Ali

My fear of the finish line has got to be the most transparent thing I have ever written in my life. I would have never thought that I, Marcia, would struggle with an inner voice about finishing. After all, looking like I have it all together most days is what a strong woman is supposed to portray, right? The dictionary describes a finish line as a line marking the end of a racecourse. Well, my life has been one constant race. I've made sure I had other options available most of the time just in case something didn't work out. In the process, I discovered that I lied to myself and believed the lies I told too. Wow, I realize now I battled rejection for more than half of my life and had become the president of my own people-pleasing committee. Allowing the inner me to measure Marcia by the world's standards and not by who God says I am. I was in a race against time only to discover I was traveling nowhere fast. Spiraling out of control, my mind, body, and spirit had no connection. This led to chaotic behaviors that caused me to live in a state of procrastination and confusion.

My life was usually full of vision, hope, dreams, and ideas. Yet, I never believed that I could accomplish a thing because of all the losses I experienced. I had multiple miscarriages, which made me feel incomplete as a woman. I lost good jobs simply because I was afraid to leave my toxic first marriage. He wasn't a bad person; he was a drug addict and loved drugs more than he loved himself. Each time I started something, good ole rejection was staring me in my face and dancing in my head, telling me I wouldn't finish it. That inner critical voice would say, *you are not good enough. No one is going to support you.* Not once did I think, with all the knowledge I had, to just get some help. I mean, I knew I needed some therapy because I was constantly tripping. I lived in a constant state of offense. Even if I made a minor accomplishment, I would find a way to sabotage my victory. Whew, now if that is not some crazy behavior, I don't know what is.

I was the nursing student who graduated Nursing school in 2000 and failed her boards two times; talk about being devastated. I later became a professional college student who dropped every class that became a challenge or I fell behind in. It got to the point where

I was placed on academic probation and lost my financial aid. Shoot, I told myself, *no problem because I'm getting way too old for this school stuff anyway. My brain just doesn't work like it used to, so why even bother?* Oh, the lies I told myself only to comfort Marcia and create more excuses. Pride is a terrible thing because, again, I could have simply asked for help. I desperately needed to accomplish my goals. My self-worth was at an all-time low for years.

I had a life-changing event happen. My current husband and I were in a rocky place. I believed that our marriage was ending, and I needed to figure this life thing out. I had already been divorced once and dreaded dealing with that again. But we made it through and will be celebrating 32 years of standing the test of time in a few months. I then realized that I had been unemployed since 2004 due to my Multiple Sclerosis diagnosis. I was physically doing great but knew things needed to change.

So, after 18 years and several failed state boards, I made the decision to take my life back. I began to study again just to see how it would go. I was petrified, so I decided I wouldn't share my test date with anyone. This time it was going to be God and me alone. If no one knew I was taking the boards again, and if

I failed (again), I'd be saved from the embarrassment. The thought of telling anyone I missed the finish line for my career pursuits made me sick to my stomach. The week before the test, I attended a prayer breakfast. It was the same breakfast that a man told me years prior, "What are you afraid of? Go back to school." So here I was again, at the same breakfast, when a prophet looked at me and said, "What if HE does it? What if GOD does it this time?" The levy inside of me broke. I cried as if someone had ripped my heart out. My stoic composure was nonexistent. I encountered God like I never had before. And after I got myself together, I wondered, *what if God really does do it for me this time*? My thoughts normally didn't begin with a question. They usually started with a self-doubt statement. My mindset was from the perspective of the inner critic. I knew this needed to change but, I was so acquainted with failures I didn't know how to sever its hold on me. But that had run its course. That next week I became Marcia L. Gibson-Ali, LPN. I was a Licensed Practical Nurse in the state of Virginia. My license is considered Compact, which gives me multi-state privileges. Always supportive, my husband and daughter planned a surprise celebration. A dear friend who has cheered for me for years showed up with gifts in her hand. Yes, I had finally done it. I had reached the finish line.

As much as I wanted to be happy, Mr. Rejection told me nobody would hire a nurse who had been out of school for 18 years and had no experience. Before obtaining my license, I was a caretaker providing hospice care to my best friend and caring for my mother-in-love, who both later passed away. Even in my health crisis of thriving with Multiple Sclerosis, I cared for anyone around me who needed nursing care, never expecting anything in return. How dare that inner voice try to minimize my victories? So again, it seemed the finish line had moved further away.

So, what did I do? I moved on to the next project. I resorted to more busy work; busyness does not always mean fruitfulness. I knew God had given me the gift of working with teens, and I can do teens with my eyes closed. I was also equipped to coach parents. My family of blended love propelled me to become a family strategist specializing in blended families. Overcoming rejection has given me the heart for daughters who have lost their moms or have dysfunctional mother/daughter relationships. This soon became my ministry. After having multiple pregnancy losses, I now have more kids than this womb could have ever carried. In 2016, I founded my 501c3 nonprofit, *Time Out for Teens,* also known as TOFT, Inc. Out of TOFT Inc, *Parenting On*

Purpose was birthed to empower parents. I did all this while struggling with my family demons, the things that had plagued me, and my bloodline. And yet, I still had my inner battle of not completing things.

As I maneuvered through 2020, the Coronavirus pandemic hit like the Titanic. Friends were rapidly dying, and that finish line just kept moving. I felt as if I could not get a grip on my life or purpose. It's a hell of a thing for other people to believe in me when I didn't believe in myself. To make matters worse, the location where my nonprofit held its meetings closed. I was left to deal with the social media world because everything was going virtual. This was way out of my league. I'm a people person who loves human interactions. However, I was clueless about social media beyond making a post on Facebook, Twitter, or Instagram. I mean, what I saw others doing online had no comparison to what I called my little unprofessional posts. I would soon learn that people are not who they post. So here I was with a struggling nonprofit, a nurse without a plan, and on the inside, I still felt as if I was dying. I was dying because I was unhappy and unfulfilled.

Ultimately, I found a nursing job in the pandemic, working in behavioral health, and life was getting better with God's favor. Although, I still struggled with completing assignments and tasks. I was just all over the place. Like many, the pandemic pushed me to a place of insomnia, and I wondered what was going on inside of me. I needed to get some answers, so I sought out therapy. I needed a therapist that would help me peel back the layers of the inner me. So, I began virtual sessions; my therapist was the bomb, but I knew there was still more. Why wasn't I happy yet? Why wasn't I fulfilled? Then the biggest fear I had hit me. I contracted Coronavirus even though I was fully vaccinated.

While quarantining, God began to speak to me. First, I named this season *the conviction of Covid*. Then, God unveiled to me a timeline of incompletes. When a pass is incomplete in football, the ball goes back to the previous spot. Next, God demonstrated how when things get tough, I run. He exposed that I had competed with myself and lost. He also showed me how I used all my energy to push others across the finish line, but I didn't see that for myself.

Before the pandemic, I asked God to give me a strategy to get additional income to support my nonprofit. The answer to that prayer birthed my food preparation business, *Out The Door Charcuterie*. I can honestly say that I never thought working with meat and cheese could be therapeutic. As I lay in bed, flat on my back, recovering from Coronavirus, my mind was racing. Yup, I felt like a failure. My quickly thriving business had come to a screeching halt. That finish line had moved again. At least that's what I thought. All I heard in my head was *no more orders. No nursing. Sis, you are done.*

My heart ached in ways words could never describe. I began to speak life to myself as I lay in a room with no television, no music, and talking to my husband through a door. I only called and texted who was necessary. I prayed daily that God would let me live because I was scared. I had already experienced five family losses to this disease in ninety days. My heart begged God not to allow my family to experience anymore. But, unfortunately, the enemy knew that fear was something I was constantly trying to overcome, and he used it against me well. My heart breaks when I think of how many races I aborted because I didn't keep going and the time I misused because fear had a chokehold on my destiny. Indeed, this was not the finish line I had been reaching for.

The truth of the matter is...

The finish line never moved. I chose to stop running. Even on the days that running wasn't in me, I made the decision not to move. I elected not to condition myself for the win. I positioned myself for defeat every time.

Procrastination assassinated my destination. After my Covid recovery, I attended my second Changing Faces Conference. And with every ounce of confidence in me, I told fear it had to go and take all of its remnants with it. I came face to face with it. I stood flat-footed and denounced all its tentacles. I spoke courage, ambition, completion, and life to everything I have been called to do. I picked up the pieces of my businesses and began to work on them. I began to get organized. I decided to reject rejection and move forward. Today Out The Door Charcuterie and More, LLC is a licensed business. TOFT and Parenting On Purpose are operational. I am a published author. I am a Behavioral Health Nurse. I survived Coronavirus, and I am here for whatever God has for me to answer *yes* to. Those days of not completing tasks are over. I have learned to encourage myself even when I have no outside support. I dare you to try it. Today I stand on Philippians 1:6, "*being confident of this, that he who began a good work in you will carry it on to completion until the day of Christ Jesus.*"

One important thing I have learned in this healing process is to keep the promises I make to myself. Finishing means I had to allow myself to feel what hurt. I am now willing to do what's necessary for my success. I matter, and you matter too.

You, the one reading this book, are the very reason I chose to finish. Every goal, dream, and aspiration is important. We were all created to solve a problem on earth. Ask yourself what problems you were created to solve? Who is waiting on you to reach the finish line to pass the torch for someone else to continue their race?

Each of us has a cheering squad. Somebody somewhere is watching and waiting on you. No matter how long it takes you to finish, just don't quit. Just keep going. Do what it takes. Show up for yourself and your family. Seek the help you need to grow through what keeps holding you back. You are worth it, and don't ever let anyone tell you that you are not. If you feel lonely and rejected, cheer for your darn self! But don't you dare give up on yourself. You matter. Reject rejection. Lose the weight of waiting. Don't ever let the fear of finishing stop you. My affirmations now are that *I am a finisher, I am an incubator, and I have things to birth.*

There is victory on the other side of fear.

Now What?

You have just traveled through the lives of twelve *fear-LESS* writers. As you have walked through each emotion, you may have had to stop and catch your breath. Walking through fear after fear may have been more than you bargained for. Maybe your intention was to tiptoe through the pages of this anthology, but the more you read, the more you found yourself in at least one of the stories. Perhaps while reading, you wept uncontrollably as you connected with the one fear that has held you in bondage for years. You found yourself linked to one or more of the writers and wondered who on earth told them your story. Or maybe you didn't identify with any of them, but as you turned each page, you came face to face with your own truth. Regardless of how you to came to know and name your fear, you're now one step closer to facing it head-on and even closer to your healing.

Not only have you taken this journey with the writers, they have journeyed with and for you as well. The pain of telling their truth and the unveiling and vulnerability did not come without a cost. The sweat and tears, the sleepless nights, the unending thoughts of throwing in the towel was never just about them. The pain they endured was to absolutely free themselves, but even more than that, it was to offer *you* the permission and opportunity to transform through your own truth.

As this part of your journey with the writers has come to an end, it is our hope that the weight of your fear is lighter. You are now on your way to your next destination of healing. Your next level will require you to be transparent in a way that you may have never experienced. Removing your fear and being authentically you may cost you friends, family, and even influence, but the freedom you will gain, the joy, and peace you find will be priceless.

We encourage you to put in the work and rest when you need to but don't stop. Speak your truth even if your voice shakes. Walk boldly and unapologetically into what God has for you. Use the courageous stories as a catalyst to removing your fear. God is on your side, and as you prepare for the next phase of your trip, He will be walking right beside you. In fact, Joshua 1:9 says, "Have I not commanded you? Be strong and courageous. Do not be frightened, and do not be dismayed, for the Lord your God is with you wherever you go."

Signed,

The Fearless Contributor to Your Change

About The Authors

Ifedayo Greenway is a mother, transformational speaker, and master life coach who is passionate about her covenant with God to impact & the world and change lives.

She works as a Corporate Investigator in the financial industry, utilizing her degree in Criminal Justice. She is also the CEO of IG & MORE (*Ife Greenway & Ministry of Real Empowerment*) LLC.

A personal development coach, Ifedayo is dedicated to helping women leverage their place of pain as momentum for forward movement; she has been featured in Huffington Post, CBS, FOX, NBC, and Shoutout Atlanta.

As a fear strategist, Ifedayo teaches others the art of living a life less impacted by fear. She is the host of *Changing Faces*, an annual empowering makeover moment that encourages women to embrace their personal change journey by seeing themselves through the eyes of purpose and not circumstances.

She is the founder of the *She Unveils* movement. In addition, she serves as a writing coach helping women accomplish their literary goals by unveiling, writing, and publishing their personal stories.

Ifedayo is a five-time author and two-time best-selling author. Other published works include inspirational writings and articles which have reached thousands of readers in various mediums, including Thrive Global & Faith Heart Magazine.

Ifedayo uses her journey to strengthen others and is committed to helping women find their authentic voice in their pursuit of transformation.

YES! YES! Yes, Change!

Connect with Ifedayo at www.igandmore.com

Kenya Allen is a mother of two adult children. She received her certification in Early Childhood Education. Kenya is a preschool educator who has been teaching for over twenty-two years. She is also a C.A.S.A. worker for Portsmouth Juvenile Courts. Kenya is very active in the church that she attends. She takes her relationship with God very seriously; she does not take for granted the blessings  that have been given to her. Kenya is a firm believer that your gifts will make room for you. Because of her relationship with Him, she can pour into others. Kenya is always willing to extend her hand to help anyone that needs it. She is an inspirational speaker who gives words of wisdom and encouragement. Kenya's ability to push others into their destiny is nothing but amazing. Kenya believes that you are what you say you are, and you have what you say you have.

Contact Kenya at: inspirationalspeaker12@gmail.com

Tahisha Pernee' Thompson is a native of Camilla, Georgia. She attended Albany State University and later married the love of her life, the late Nelson James Thompson. From that union came two beautiful daughters, Jada Danielle and Jami'yah Nicole.

Tahisha worked ten years with the Department of Defense. A strong tug towards cooking compelled her to become the owner of A Sweet Taste of Heaven LLC.

After losing her husband unexpectedly, Tahisha became an advocate for women struggling to find life after death or divorce. Learning to accept a new norm, Tahisha founded *Freely Embracing Me, a community where s*he focuses on the importance of self-love & self-care. As a Freedom Coach, she equips and encourages others by relating her painful past experiences to her newfound freedom. Her innovative way of transparency has changed lives all over the world. Tahisha has survived much to qualify for this season of her life.

Contact Tahisha at: tahishathompson@gmail.com

Nicki Peacock is a Master Stylist, Makeup Artist, and Motivational Speaker. She is the owner of The Peacock Experience in Chesapeake, Virginia. Priding herself on being a "tattooed disciple," she uses her gift of communicating God's word to transform lives. Encouraging people worldwide, her passion is helping women to reclaim their self-worth by embracing the essence of their feathers  and seeing their beauty from the inside out. Working with Nicki Peacock is more than an encounter; it's an experience.

Contact Nicki Peacock at: thepeacockexperience@gmail.com

Arlene Kidd is a native of Hamilton, New Jersey. She is the youngest of four children who grew up in the same household: two sisters and one brother by way of her mother and two older brothers by way of her father. She is a proud mother of three adult children and two grandchildren. The State of New Jersey has employed her for over 32 years. She has a great love for helping others and does it through her diligence in getting benefits paid to those who are temporarily disabled. She also has a love for the elderly. She has dabbled in the capacity as a companion care worker to be the caregiver to those who may not be capable of caring for themselves. She has a passion for opening an adult day center and a hair salon one day.

Contact Arlene at: born2praz50@gmail.com

Alva Kershaw is a native of Richmond, Virginia, and a mother of two beautiful daughters. She received her undergraduate degree from the University of Virginia, Masters of Social Work (M.S.W.) from Virginia Commonwealth University, and Masters of Divinity (M. Div.) from Virginia Union University.

Alva is a licensed clinical social worker (LCSW) and an ordained pastor. Through her work and passion as a therapist, she developed Touchstone Counseling Services, providing outpatient therapy, psycho-education, coaching, energy healing, and professional development. The mission of Touchstone Counseling Services is to serve as a catalyst to help community members reach their goals and highest potential.

Connect with Alva at: www.touchstonerva.com

Sandra L. Parker is the founder and visionary of Speak Life on Purpose, LLC., a movement designed to empower women to embrace a "think different, speak different" mindset.

Focusing on her life experiences, Sandra encourages women to embrace change and access their power to grow. She has a strong desire to see women turn their pain into positive growth. As a mindset coach, she aims to help women move from a fixed mindset to a growth mindset.

Sandra believes that God's mandate as it concerns women is to encourage, motivate and inspire them to demolish old mindsets and to provide them with affirming tools that empowers them to use their authentic voice to Speak Life over every area of their lives regardless of their circumstances.

Sandra is a mother of one daughter, a licensed minister, a certified professional life and mindset coach, a best-selling author, and a transformational speaker.

Connect with Sandra at: www.speaklifeonpurpose.com

Shannon Nicole is the self-published author of *Stop Crying & Use Your Words* and *Stop Crying & Use Your Words FOR KIDS*. She is an educator by trade and has worked in the field of education since 2001, serving at-risk populations and students with disabilities, and the general population. Shannon uses her gifts of writing and oration to "*start conversations for you and God to finish.*" Her greatest  joy is helping people move in the direction of God's calling for their lives. She enjoys traveling, music, movies, and laughing. Loving her husband and children is her highest honor and privilege. Shannon earned a Bachelor of Science degree in communication from Old Dominion University in Norfolk, Virginia, and trained in executive leadership and administration. She resides in Florida with her husband Jason, daughter Riley, and dog Milo. Shannon also loves two bonus adult sons, Jason and Eric.

Contact Shannon at: shannonjohnson119@gmail.com

Mavis Rowe, LCSW, is a native of Portsmouth, VA. Her motto is, "If you don't like something, change it. If you can't change it, change your attitude."-Maya Angelou. Mavis is a licensed clinical social worker who currently works with the geriatric community and has over twelve years of experience in mental health. She holds a master's degree in social work and is pursuing a second master's in divinity. She's passionate about empowering women to excel beyond the social and political constraints that bind them. Mavis is a proud wife and mother of 6 adult children. She is a member of The Mount at Chesapeake. She is involved with Summit Wellness, where she assists the executive director and facilitates small groups. She is also a new author, and her first book, "They're Gone. Now What?: A Grief Journey from Self-torment to Soul-Transformation," is scheduled to be released in March of 2022.

Contact Mavis at: m.rowe.lcsw@gmail.com

Mother, international preacher, leadership consultant, certified life coach, author, mentor, and founder of Women Empowered in the Millennium and The Empowerment Circle, **Dr. Angela Corprew-Boyd** is a change agent who empowers others to fulfill their destinies. Author of two books, _If I Perish, Let Me Perish, But I'm Next_ and _Church Hurt: The Wounded Trying to Heal,_ she also hosts the _Empowerment with Dr. Angie_ talk show, which celebrates the work of

women and motivates viewers by sharing words of empowerment. Dr. Corprew-Boyd earned her doctorate in strategic leadership from Regent University and served in Chesapeake Public Schools for 30 years as a teacher, assistant principal, and human resources administrator. She has also worked as an academic vice-principal in the United Arab Emirates and in leadership with Cornerstone International Church. In addition, she immensely loves parenting three adult children and grandchildren.

Connect with Dr. Angie at: www.angieboydministries.org

This is where I am supposed to try and woo and impress you with my credentials and so forth. Well, that really isn't my style. My days of being phony and superficial are over. But what I can tell you about myself is the following:

- **Monique Jewell Anderson** is a classy, straight shooter

- I love to laugh, and I'm pretty funny

- I love to dance, and my guilty musical pleasure is vibing out to Nelly

- I have five children- I didn't necessarily pray for five kids, but the Lord blessed me beyond what I knew I needed with each of them.

- I am married to the absolute love of my life; if I knew back then what I know now, I would have waited my entire life to meet him.

- I have one grandson, and yes, he is my everything, and he knows it.

- I love God, and He loves me right back, and there ain't a thing I can do to make Him change His mind about me.

- And oh, I am a 3x author, an excellent publisher (Spirit Filled Creations LLC) with celebrity, mega-church pastors, educators, judges, and moms as clients.

- I have a deep passion for millennials and future generations.

- I am a puSHEr, and I'm equipped to push people, to push YOU, to reach your full potential.

Connect with Monique at: www.spiritfilledcreations.com

Marcia Ali is a native of Newark, NJ. She is a talented writer, licensed nurse, and the owner of Out The Door Charcuterie & More.

Marcia is the CEO and founder of TOFT (Time Out For Teens), a 501c3 nonprofit and Parenting On Purpose. With over 25 years of experience, she is an advocate who is souled-out for families. She attributes that passion to her journey of having a teenage son sentenced to 18 years in prison.

As a teenologist, Marcia pulls greatness out of every teen and parent she encounters across the nation. She empowers & encourages them to be intentional in their relationships.

Now residing in Suffolk, VA, with her husband, they share an immense amount of love for six children and their grandchildren. They consider their family to be a reflection of blended love! In addition, Marcia offers a variety of consulting services.

Contact Marcia at: marciaali757@gmail.com